WALKING FORWARD

USING THE POWER OF HABIT TO NAVIGATE THE CHAOS OF LIFE
... one step at a time

Shawn —
Cheers to long hikes!
xo Sarah.

Copyright @ 2023 Sarah Hepburn

Walking Forward: Using the Power of Habit to Navigate the Chaos of Life . . . One Step at a Time

YGTMedia Co. Trade Paperback Edition.

ISBN trade paperback: 978-1-998754-10-6

eBook: 978-1-998754-11-3

All Rights Reserved. No part of this book can be scanned, distributed, or copied without permission. This book or any portion thereof may not be reproduced or used in any manner whatsoever without the express written permission of the publisher at publishing@ygtmedia.co—except for the use of brief quotations in a book review.

The author has made every effort to ensure the accuracy of the information within this book was correct at time of publication. The author does not assume and hereby disclaims any liability to any party for any loss, damage, or disruption caused by errors or omissions, whether such errors or omissions result from accident, negligence, or any other cause.

This book is designed to provide information and motivation to our readers. It is sold with the understanding that the publisher is not engaged to render any type of psychological, legal, or any other kind of professional advice. The content is the sole expression and opinion of its author, and not necessarily that of the publisher. No warranties or guarantees are expressed or implied by the publisher's choice to include any of the content in this book. Neither the publisher nor the author shall be liable for any physical, psychological, emotional, financial, or commercial damages, including, but not limited to, special, incidental, consequential or other damages. Our views and rights are the same: You are responsible for your own choices, actions, and results.

Published in Canada, for Global Distribution by YGTMedia Co.

www.ygtmedia.co/publishing

To order additional copies of this book: publishing@ygtmedia.co

Edited by Kelly Lamb

Book design by Doris Chung

Cover design by Michelle Fairbanks

ePub edition by Ellie Sipilä

Author Photo: Photography by Nat Caron

TORONTO

WALKING FORWARD

USING THE POWER OF HABIT
TO NAVIGATE THE CHAOS OF LIFE
. . . one step at a time

sarah hepburn.

To Brad, I will always love you.

To my boys, Noah, Zach, and Cooper, you are the greatest gifts I never knew I needed and my best, most loved teachers. I am grateful to be part of your story in life.

contents

PROLOGUE: FOOTPRINTS OF LIFE 1

INTRODUCTION: ONE FOOT IN FRONT OF THE OTHER 3

HABITS ARE FREEING 9

YOUR IDENTITY 49

UNLOCKING THE POWER OF HABITS 79

SIMPLICITY 111

CONSISTENCY 135

ACCOUNTABILITY 157

LIFE HAPPENS 183

HABITS PROVIDE CALM IN CHAOS 203

WALKING FORWARD 209

WITH GRATITUDE (A.K.A. ACKNOWLEDGMENTS) 219

RESOURCES AND WORKS CITED 223

PROLOGUE

footprints of life

Why write a book?

Will anyone read it? Why bother sharing anything I've learned with others?

The short answer? Because everyone has a story that matters. It is just that simple.

For the longest time, I didn't think anyone would care what I had to say.

I thought my life was average and unfolding along a predictable path. Graduate high school and university, get a job, get married, buy a house, have kids . . . ride off into the sunset?

It all seemed so prescribed. So . . . inevitable.

Until one day I started to write my "boring" stories down. At first, I wrote for myself. I wrote as a way to remember. As a way to understand. As a way to find my voice like I never had before. The more I wrote, the more confident I became. I started to untangle stories I had told myself.

The more I wrote, the more I realized I had things to say.

When I started sharing a few of my stories as a personal blog, people actually read them! Not only did they read them, but they would reach out and tell me things they identified with.

I didn't know others felt that way.
I thought I was the only one.
I learned something today.

I kept writing. I kept sharing. I came to realize that in sharing pieces of my story, others felt like their story mattered too. I found a connection with others through common experience.

This book is about how I've used the power of habit consciously and unconsciously to navigate chaos in my life. It is how I have found clarity and figured out what I want my life to look like. It is full of personal stories with actionable takeaways for you, the reader. There are tools on my website you can download and use again and again as you power up your own habits to find calm amid the chaos in life.

I hope you will find nuggets here and there on how **you can use habits to walk forward in the story of your life.**

INTRODUCTION

one foot in front of the other . . .

"A journey of a thousand miles begins with a single step."
–Chinese proverb

Some thirty years later, I was back in Scotland. I had been there once before, for an international synchronized swimming competition as an eighteen-year-old. The event was held in Glasgow, and to be honest, I don't remember much about the country except a day trip to Edinburgh and an adventure on the local bus system trying to find a Catholic church in very Protestant Scotland so one of my teammates could attend her weekly Mass. We were too busy having fun as a team to take in the sights. I definitely remember the Scottish accents, though. Just as thick as everyone said they would be.

Now, as a wife, mother, and full-fledged adult, I was back in the gorgeous country. My husband and I wanted an active holiday, and for the first time, we weren't constrained by the kids' plans as they were all either at camp or working. After some research, we decided to walk the West Highland Way, a 154 km trek that stretched from just outside Glasgow in the south to Fort William farther north.

I was beyond excited about our trip. I spent the months leading up to it making sure I was getting hikes in on the local trails each week. I worked on my leg and core strength so I could navigate the ups and downs and uneven terrain. I researched and planned all the details. Travel logistics, equipment needs, food. You name it, I probably had a list for it.

Our Scotland trip came on the heels of a busy season of life. Our older boys were graduating high school; our youngest, grade eight. My husband had a ton of work-related deadlines, and I was racing to finish the first draft of this book. There were family events and weekends away with friends. It was a wonderful and very full few weeks.

Leaving the chaos of home behind, en route to Glasgow, we spent the weekend in Halifax celebrating a friend's fiftieth birthday. It was a weekend filled with laughs, old friends, live music, lots of drinks, and little sleep. By the time we arrived in Milngavie, the town where the West Highland Way begins, we were exhausted. A perfect way to start a seven-day, 154 km trek, right? Spoiler: no!

We set out on our first day bright and early. The guidebook promised a fairly easy 19 km walk to kick things off. I would love to write that all my preparation in the months leading up to this day paid off, but the truth is the first day on the trail was not my best. I was really tired. I was hot. My backpack was uncomfortable. My hip hurt. I was winded and walking super slow. Basically, I was a salty mess. My husband even took a picture to poke fun at how grumpy I was. I look at it now and laugh at the expression on my face. But I wasn't impressed at the time when he took it!

I got through the day and heaved a sigh of relief as I took my hiking boots off. I was ready for a hot meal, a warm shower, and an early night. Day two was completely different. My energy was refreshed, and I was ready to go. We hiked up the hills beside Loch Lomond. We walked among lush green ferns, past waterfalls. We listened to the water lapping at the shore. We ate dinner at a different pub each night and recounted the day with giggles and pride.

By day four, we had found our groove. We were now deep in the Scottish Highlands walking through Rannoch Moor and into Glencoe where centuries ago Scottish clansmen fought, and more recently, where the James Bond movie *Skyfall* was filmed. The land was wild, and the scenery outstanding as we navigated the old military paths along our route.

There was a simplicity to our days: wake up, eat breakfast, walk, pause, walk some more. Each day ended at the pub followed by a warm shower and falling into bed at night. One foot in front of the other, step by step, we moved forward. We knew where we were headed, and we took turns cheering each other on when we needed to.

On our second last day, I could feel the sniffles starting. It was the shortest day of our trek at only 14 km long, but I hadn't slept well the night before and every step felt heavy and labored. At lunch, we lingered longer than usual, and I closed my eyes and had a trailside nap. I woke feeling refreshed and ready to continue. The scenery continued to shine, and we celebrated at the pub at the day's end. Once in our hotel room, I took some extra vitamin C, added some more supplements, and popped a few Tylenol to help with the achy feelings. Most of all, I didn't get mad at my body. In fact, I spent a few minutes with my journal writing about how proud I was of how it had carried me this far.

On our final day on the trail, it was hot and the sun was relentless with no shade on the wide open paths. Scotland was having an "unprecedented" heat wave, and no one had prepared for hiking in 30-degree-plus weather! I was still feeling crappy but eager to get going and see what the day had to offer as we trekked our final 24 km. As we rounded the corner near the end of the day, Ben Nevis, the highest point in the United Kingdom, soared into view. It was thrilling. We both paused, feeling a huge sense of accomplishment. Any sniffles and aches I was feeling faded as I stood and celebrated the moment.

I learned a lot on that trip:

- I learned that preparation pays off. I never would have been able to complete the trek if I hadn't continued my training plan during the busy month leading up to our departure.
- I learned that just because you have one bad day on the trail doesn't mean you are going to have two.
- I learned that pausing and having a nap, even in the middle of a hiking day, makes a world of difference.

- I learned that I can do things to help my body recover along the way.
- I learned that hiking—like life—is truly one step at a time.
- And I was reminded life isn't meant to be lived alone. The encouragement and humor from my husband are what got me through the hard spots.

These are some of the lessons I'm going to share with you in this book. With a little clarity and consistent steps forward, you, too, will be able to navigate the chaos of life. Let's get started!

habits are freeing

> "Habits have enabled me to find calm when life feels chaotic."
> –Sarah Hepburn

Some habits, like brushing my teeth, I learned at an early age. My mom taught me how to hold a toothbrush, how long to brush for, and which direction to move the bristles as a toddler. Now, as an adult, it's automatic. How many of us think about our technique when we brush our teeth?

Other habits, like applying makeup, I acquired over time. I keep my makeup in a toiletry bag on the bathroom counter. When I'm getting ready in the morning, I start by taking everything I need out of the bag and placing it on the counter. Then, as I use each product, I put the item back in the bag. For me, this habit means that I know what I have already used and what I still need to do. I don't have to pause and wonder if I have already applied deodorant!

Brushing your teeth, putting on makeup, and tying your shoes are all examples of daily habits that many of us do without thought. For me, habits are behaviors that have not only helped me function with basic life routines, but they're also tools I have leveraged to enable positive change or provide stability.

For example, many years ago, we went on a family heli-hiking trip. I was so excited about the adventure but was in the worst physical shape of my life. The added pressure was that my youngest son, who was a year and a half at the time, would be carried in a hiking backpack for a lot of the trek. And he was particular about who carried him: Momma! This meant I had to whip myself into shape. I had to commit to daily movement to achieve my goal. I had to build the habit. At first, it was hard. But I started small. And I was consistent. I kept showing up each day, and bit by bit, my strength grew. The trip has long since passed, but physical activity has remained a cornerstone of my daily life. And that hiking trip is easily one of the most memorable experiences of my life.

> ***When life feels chaotic around me, I rely on my daily habits for a sense of comfort and stability.***

Pandemic-land put my daily routine to the test. When schools were closed and we were all at home, everything felt topsy-turvy. At the start, it was hard to stay motivated. The urge to stay in pajamas all day was strong. It felt pointless to go to bed at a consistent time or wake up early and journal like I usually do. But after mourning what life was like "before," I was able to find stability in my daily routine. In doing so, it strengthened my ability to weather the various pandemic punches that just kept coming.

In our family at one point, I was the repository for everyone's schedules, planner of all meals, and manager of the house. My brain was ready to explode. Now, we have a centrally located whiteboard that everyone refers to so they know what is happening when (mostly without asking me!). They all have a dedicated place to put their crap when they come home. Meal planning has never been my strength, but I added a basic outline of dinners for the week and the kids, now that they are older, are helping to brainstorm ideas and sometimes even prep food. Implementing these systems and habits has enabled our family to talk about things we want to instead of yelling at each other because of miscommunication.

Regular, predictable daily habits can seem boring, mundane, blah. But they aren't. Habits and routines that are created intentionally establish a foundation that enables us to live our best lives. A deliberately crafted set of daily habits helps me do more of what I want with the people I love.

It is the moments when I'm distracted that things seem to go sideways. The moments when I turn my brain off and my body keeps moving, irrespective of what is in front of me. Sometimes, it's as simple as tripping over a tree root while hiking. I have walked into doors because I was talking and not paying attention. Bruised ego, perhaps a bruised knee from falling, but often nothing more would come from some of my mental diversion.

There have been times, though, when the consequences of my

distraction have been a little more than I bargained for. Shit will happen in life. It just will. All the best-laid plans can go awry in a nanosecond. But what I also know is that **it is what you do when times are calm and stable that makes a difference when chaos happens.**

When I slowed down long enough to listen, when I was intentional with what I was doing and not distractedly running through life, I was able to get clear on what worked for me. Not what worked for others. Not what I should be doing. Not what was expected of me. But clarity on what I wanted.

I came to understand that expecting nothing to happen just isn't how life goes. Crap will happen. Once I accepted that chaos is a given, I was able to focus on what was in my control.

I started to build habits that were focused on a healthy body and mind. Movement every day and quality sleep at night were key. I started small and walked every day for at least thirty minutes. This was something I was able to do consistently, and it helped build on my movement goals over time. Through walking, I was able to slow life down. I felt calm. I did—and still do—my best thinking when I'm walking. There is something about the rhythm of putting one foot in front of the other that helps calm the chaos around me.

I also worked to understand more about my body, what I could do to bolster my immune system, what supplements would help, and importantly, what I could do to minimize the effects of an allergic reaction or any health event. I worked on my mindset and my mental health. Years of wobbly physical health had taken their toll on my mental health, and

I had grown increasingly anxious about what would go wrong next and skeptical about what I was able to achieve in life.

As I understood more about myself, why I behaved how I did, and what it was that I wanted, I began to develop habits that worked for me. Knowing what I wanted meant that I was able to sustain my new habits.

With consistent forward progress, I have come to find kindness and forgiveness for my body along with a level of gratitude for what I can do that I never had before. Habits have been the tools that I used to move forward. Habits have been the tools that I use to find stable footing when the inevitable hiccups in life occur. Sinus colds on holiday. Family issues. And even everyday interruptions.

I haven't always been so aware of how habits have shaped me, but I know that I've always thrived when I have habits and routines in my life that work. **I realized that habits have always enabled me to find calm when life feels chaotic.**

I share in this book how habits have carried me forward in good times and helped me get through the not-so-good times. I share how you can leverage the power of habit, too, to enable you to craft a life that is intentional and serves you. It takes slowing down and paying attention. It also takes reflection and action.

I'll add prompts throughout (under the heading Footprints) for you to reflect upon. I'm hoping they will encourage you to take the steps needed to walk forward with calm confidence. **Life can be chaotic without a plan, but by approaching it one step at a time, you'll find your footing and your focus.**

If you were to use habits more strategically, what change could you bring to your life? Are you ready to find out?

KNOWING WHAT HABITS WILL WORK FOR YOU

Knowing what you need first starts with knowing yourself. Who have you been in the past? Who are you now? Be really honest. Knowing yourself isn't something that you sit down and make a list as if you are going grocery shopping. It's a process. It is peeling back the layers—and it can be hard. If you start to track the patterns in your life that got you to where you are today, they will inform how you can shape what you want your life to look like tomorrow.

Once you have a better picture of where you have been and where you want to go, take an inventory of what you want to change to move forward. Change doesn't happen just because you wish it. Deliberate, intentional, consistent shifts in how you do things each day are the levers that will move you in the direction you want.

WANDERING THROUGH LIFE

One night I had a vivid dream. It was so real that when I woke in the morning my legs felt tired as if they had been walking all night.

I was crossing a series of long bridges. Some were wooden, like old railway bridges. Some were suspension bridges over giant canyons of rushing water. Others were massive concrete bridges crossing freeways and roads full of traffic. At times, the wind would howl and the bridge would sway back and forth. I grabbed the guardrail to steady myself. Other times, the air was still, but the relentless heat from the hot sun made walking dizzying.

There were other people on the bridges, and I would smile as we passed. They didn't seem as concerned about getting to the other side as I was. They were looking at the view. Posing for pictures. Staring at the cloud patterns in the sky. I would take their pictures when they handed me their camera. I smiled and nodded. I even acknowledged the windy or hot or rainy weather to them as I moved along. You know, being polite, ha.

These people actually got in my way as I tried to rush past. I could feel the flicker of annoyance bubble inside me when I couldn't move as quickly as I wanted. They were getting in my way of where I wanted to go. Why were they lingering and taking their time? Why didn't they care about getting to the other side and moving quicker?

I was frustrated but also curious why I was so focused on getting across and they didn't seem to care.

In my dream, I never got to the other side of the bridge. I would cross one bridge and it would lead directly onto another bridge. I could hear the rushing water of the river as I was crossing one; the hum of traffic below another. I could see mountains from one bridge and felt surrounded by nature, while other times, it was a slog to keep moving over a bridge crossing a dried-up creek or a desolate road.

I started to notice that I was now by myself on the bridges. The people who had been lingering and taking their time were no longer there. When I first noticed this, I wasn't sure how to feel. I kept moving forward from bridge to bridge. Always different, but always the same.

I was going nowhere. Never reaching my destination.

I was all alone.

What if I stopped? What would happen?
As I approached the middle of a swaying suspension bridge, I nervously paused. Everything seemed so unstable. My stomach dipped each time the bridge moved in a wave with the wind. I closed my eyes, gripped the handrail, and took a deep breath. Right in the middle, I stopped. I was the farthest from either side. I could barely see where the bridge started and where it ended.

I stood there. All alone. No one to help me. No one to show me where to go. No route to guide me. **The only way to find the path was if I stopped long enough to notice where I was and get clear on what direction I wanted to go next.** I had to figure that out on my own.

My path. My life. My bridge. I could feel my eyes opening as I understood where I stood.

In the middle of the swaying suspension bridge, I felt the wind on my cheeks. I could hear the rushing water blasting over the rocks in the canyon way below me. The sky was a bright blue and the towering pines a dark green.

I stood there. I paused. I felt the power of nature all around me.

I stopped moving long enough to notice where I was, acknowledge where I had been, and set my eyes toward where I could go.

I stopped moving long enough to allow myself to catch my breath. To pause. To observe. To listen. It was scary. It was beautiful. It transformed me.

As I stood there, I started to notice others around me again. I wasn't alone. There were other people sharing what they had done and where they had come from. Each knowing they could choose their own path but also recognizing that they needed help from others along the way.

At that moment, I knew that whatever path I chose would be the right one—because it was my path. My life. I had paused. I had stopped rushing. I was able to choose. To see what was all around me. I finally had clarity.

With a deep breath and a smile on my face, I started moving again. I stepped off the bridge. Curious to see what was on the other side and knowing that I was meant to be there.

footprints.

→ *Have you ever felt like you were wandering through life?*
→ *Have you ever had a dream so vivid that it seems real?*
→ *What do you think it meant?*

WHO DO YOU WANT TO BE?

My workout routine transformed when I decided that I was a fit person. That's just who I am.

I have always done my best work and have been at my best when there is a predictable routine in my daily life. Habits like making my bed each morning cue me to start the day and get going. Creating a home where everything has a place has helped contain the chaos not only of three kids but also the chaos in my brain. If I wanted to make a change, such as exercising more, I would try to figure out a way to incorporate movement into my daily life so that it was more than just a passing idea.

For me, it boiled down to a very simple concept. You can say that you want to do something, but if you don't have a plan on how you're going to get there, it will be harder to do the things that you want. **You can choose to take charge of your life—or you can sit back and let life happen to you.**

Things will get hard along the way to achieving a goal or doing something that you want. Habits are established when times are stable, and habits support you when things get tough. A well-established habit is working when it becomes another daily action you take without having to think about it. It is just something you do. It is part of who you are.

Too often habits are thought of as a bad habit or something to change. "I need to stop eating chips" or "I drink too much Diet Coke" or "I need to stop bingeing Netflix." While this is true, I like to think about habits as something to leverage. Habits—when formed with intention—can be powerful! For example, I want to do an eight-day, two-hundred-kilometer trek this summer. I need to be in good shape to do this. My identity is as a fit woman in her late forties who loves to hike. So I ask myself, what are the habits of a woman who loves to hike?

Well, she walks daily. She thinks about her nutrition in terms of fueling her body. She lifts weights. She is consistent in all these things. She doesn't just plan to work out each day, she does it because that is just what she does. It is who she is. Working out is part of her identity. Hiking is part of her identity, and her habits are aligned with who she is.

It wasn't always this way. I would often start and stop working out. I would dream of being super fit but lose momentum once I started. I always had big plans to do things, but they wouldn't always work out. It all just seemed too overwhelming, so I'd give up. What was the tipping point where habits finally stuck for me?

There were four things that made the difference:

My identity

I decided that I was a person who was fit, even if I didn't feel like it at the time. Being fit was just who I was. Every time I didn't want to work out, I reminded myself of who I was. I dressed the part by putting my gym clothes on first thing in the morning in preparation for my workout.

Timing

I always worked out in the morning. I learned that if I didn't workout first thing in the morning, the workout didn't happen because the noise of the day got in the way. After a while it just became part of my morning routine. It became automatic, so I didn't have to think about it.

Accountability

When I was establishing my daily exercise habit, I signed up for an online fitness program. Even though the workouts were pre-recorded and online, it felt like the instructor was yelling at me in person to "go, go, go!" I was able to track my progress through the app. In theory, no one took attendance, but the combination of his energy on the screen and reaching milestones through the app made me want to keep going.

Practicality

I set up a small gym in our home. Before I had a gym at home (and by gym, I mean a few sets of weights and a mat—it doesn't need to be complicated!), I basically paid rent to the gym nearby. I would sign up for a membership and rarely go because by the time I got there for an hour class and back home again, it would be two hours. That's a lot in a day.

Now, I set my gym clothes out the night before so I can't avoid them, and I head downstairs to work out in the morning. My workouts are between thirty and forty-five minutes, and bam, I am done. Making it easy to do was a game changer for me.

When I don't feel like working out, which, to be totally honest, happens at times, I start by getting dressed. If I am in my gym clothes already I have a much higher likelihood of heading downstairs to start the workout. If I make it downstairs and start working out, I think, *well, I'm already here, I may as well keep going.* And before I know it, my workout is done, and I feel mentally and physically better.

Building up my identity, figuring out the best time to exercise, creating some form of accountability, and making it easy to do and hard to avoid have been key in starting and keeping my habit of working out daily.

Now, I move my body every day because I am a fit person. That is who I am.

footprints.

- ➤ Who do you want to be? For example, I wanted to be a fit person.
- ➤ What habits will help you achieve that?
- ➤ What do you think is holding you back from who you want to be?

WRITING THE STORY OF YOU

What if you could write your own story? What would you say? How do you want people to remember you? Where would you even start?

Over the years, I've felt like no one really knew me. No one really understood who I was on the inside. There was swimmer Sarah. There was party girl Sarah. There was Sarah, the mom of twins. There was Sarah, Brad's wife. John and Barb's daughter. One of the Hepburn girls. The list went on.

I suppose that, as a society, we are more comfortable assigning labels to people. It is a way others can relate to us. I get it. I do the same thing. But over time, you can feel like the real you is screaming on the inside to get out, and you don't even know where to start.

I'm a relatively private person, and it can take a while to get to know me. I have never been particularly comfortable talking about myself with others, and my instinct is to direct the conversation in a different direction. I have wondered why I do this. Part of it is that I am keenly interested in what others are doing, and I love hearing the stories others have to share. But there has been an element over the years of not being totally comfortable in my own skin. And over time, it became easier to carry the labels that others assigned me.

When I started to ask myself what I really wanted, it became clear that to be able to answer that question, I first had to understand more about who I was first. What do I know about Sarah? Why do I think and react the way I do? What am I like in relationships? How do I reset? How do I talk to myself? Once I started asking with intent, the questions seemed endless. Just as I am curious to talk to others about their own stories, I became curious about my own.

THE CABIN IN THE WOODS

What if the vision for your future comes to you in a way that is totally unexpected and yet so powerful you can't ignore what you have seen? There is a vision that has appeared to me a number of times during my morning meditation sessions. I don't know what it means or where it takes place, but I have chills each time it comes to me. It is so real. So aligned. It feels so me.

> *I was standing in a field on a sunny day. The sky was a brilliant blue marked by wisps of white clouds moving high in the sky above me. I could feel the grass on my ankles. It was damp still from the overnight dew. The wildflowers were in full bloom, and as I looked around I saw pockets of purple and yellow standing bright against the dark green grass. The mountains rose up to surround the field where I stood, making me feel small and on top of the world all at once.*
>
> *I turned my gaze toward the woods down below where I stood. There was a small cottage at the edge of the forest. It was a log cabin that looked both cozy and spacious. I started to walk through the grass toward it. My long skirt grazed the wet grass, and I could feel the squish of the soft ground under my feet. As I got closer to the*

cabin, I could see the warm glow of the lights inside. There were several rose bushes on one side of the house and a massive vegetable garden on the other. The raised beds were overflowing with fresh produce. In a quick glance, I could see a variety of lettuces, tomatoes, vines of zucchini and cucumber, and what looked to be some watermelons too. My practical brain briefly wondered how this magical garden hadn't been destroyed by snacking deer, but that thought left as quickly as it had come.

I didn't know who lived in this log cabin, but I knew I needed to find out. As I walked up the path, I felt nervous. Maybe this was a mistake, I thought. I lifted my hand to knock on the door and it opened before I had a chance to tap. There, in front of me, stood an older woman. She had long flowing gray hair. She had a warm smile and eyes that welcomed me forward. She was barefoot and wore a light summer dress that skimmed her fit body. As she invited me in, I tried not to stare but it was hard—she seemed so familiar.

She asked if I would like a cup of tea, and I noticed the table had been set for two. She was expecting me, I realized. We sat together, mostly in silence, and hugged our warm mugs and ate the sweet scones dripping in butter she shared with me. After some time, I stood to leave knowing that I needed to keep walking before darkness set in. She smiled and told me she was so happy I had come. As I hugged her goodbye, I could feel an energy between us. There was a deep connection that was both unexpected and welcome.

As I walked back down the path from her cottage I turned and looked to see her standing in the doorway. Her long hair blew softly *in the breeze. She waved and smiled. At that moment I realized that I had just met my future self. I had just met a woman who was calm and confident and totally at peace with herself. I have no idea where this cottage was or what mountains I was surrounded by, but I knew I would never forget that moment.*

As I write these words, the chills return. How can I ignore the signs my physical body is sending my heart and mind? What am I meant to do with this information? This place. This feeling. Is this it? Am I meant to seek out this cottage and this woman? I am not sure. What if that is where I am meant to be?

I think about this vision often. I think about the calm, kind, wise woman I met. I wonder how she got there? I wonder what her life had been like leading up to that moment.

I have more questions than answers, but it is an intuitive knowing that somewhere in my future I will stand in a cottage just like the one in my vision.

footprints.

➤ Have you ever had a vision like I shared? What did it look like?

➤ Pretend you are having tea with your future self. Write about this encounter. Where was it? What did you talk about?

➤ Lots of people have opinions about your life—but it is your life not theirs. If you were to write a list of things you know about yourself, what would it say?

ASKING QUESTIONS

Who am I? This is a question I think about often. A mother. A wife. A sister. A daughter. A friend. I am also a writer. A designer. A hiker. A curious person. I love to read. I love to travel and meet new people (this is starting to sound like a dating profile!). The point is that in one day, one hour, one minute, you can be so many things as a vibrant human. That's what is awesome about our lives—we can be so many things. A fact that is both freeing and incredibly confusing all at the same time.

    I was thirty when I became a mother. Throughout my twenties, I had more or less cruised through life. I moved through each day reacting to whatever happened. At the time, motherhood was an identity I wasn't sure I was ready to assume. When the boys were born, the nurses and doctors referred to me as "Mom," never Sarah. I get that it made it easy for them not to have to know my name, but it only added to all the "what the heck had happened to Sarah?" feelings I was experiencing.

As time went on, the busyness of life took over. If I thought I had cruised through my twenties, my thirties were a haze of sleepless nights, racing from one thing to another, and never really feeling like I had any say in what was happening in my life. I just kept going. Never stopped.

As my kids got a bit older and I got more sleep, I started to wonder if this was really IT in life. What would happen when they didn't need me as much? What was I doing with work and my career? I liked it, sort of. Increasingly, however, I was more irritated with work than I was passionate about what I was doing.

It was at this point that the voice started to whisper. It was easy to ignore at first. The whisper. The signs. The knowing. Nothing was particularly broken—and life was good—but I knew in my heart that there was more.

This first step of self-awareness would set me on a path to where I am today. It all started with the intuitive feeling that there was more for me in life and, after a lot of steps forward and backward, a determination to be intentional in how I lived. Stop the drift. Live life on my own terms.

What did this look like? How did I work through the understanding of myself to determine what I wanted out of life? I would love to say it was a linear five-step process, but that couldn't be further from the truth. It started as a constant gnawing. A persistent voice in my head that was wondering. It wasn't until I took time away, just for myself, that things really started to shift. I started to peel back the layers that had built up over the years to understand how the events of the past had shaped me into the person I am today.

I thought back to what I was like as a young girl. What did I do? What did I like? What was ten-year-old Sarah like? I started to understand how I was getting in my own way. I started to understand that it mattered how I talked to myself. I really wasn't very nice to myself!

This all sounds simple and easy to do, but it is a process that takes patience and trust. Trust in knowing that things will happen if you open yourself to possibility. Trust in knowing that you cannot control what goes on around you. Trust in knowing that there will be hard days, but they will make the good all that much better.

Most of all, **trust to love yourself enough to live a life that you will look back on and be proud of.**

footprints.

- ➔ *Have you felt the nudge that there might be something more for you?*
- ➔ *Think back to when you were young. What did you dream about?*
- ➔ *Now, pretend you are at the end of your life. Are you proud of the life you've lived?*

MY FIRST HOUSE

Do you remember the first house you lived in? I do.

We lived on a quiet street in the west end of Toronto. There were a ton of kids my age, and we would spend our days roaming the streets on our bikes and going to the park. There were endless games of hide and seek running between the backyards, and we knew we could count on neighbors to open their doors if we needed anything. It was an idyllic and special neighborhood.

The house faced west and was shaded from the afternoon sun by the massive tree in the front yard. When you entered, you were greeted by the living room to your left, the dining room to your right, and the stairs to the second floor just ahead. I remember friends gathering around the dining room table for my birthday parties, family holiday occasions in the living room, and quiet evenings with my mom and sister eating dinner in the kitchen when my dad was working late. My favorite meal was mac 'n' cheese with cut-up hot dogs mixed in. Gross!

Upstairs, my bedroom was at the front of the house next to the bathroom. I loved that room and spent hours in there. I don't recall what it looked like, but I remember where the bed was positioned on the wall and the long dresser that sat opposite it. Mostly I remember it being cozy and organized. My parents had a little sitting area and a TV in their bedroom across the hall, and we curled up there watching Lady Diana and Prince Charles get married super early one July morning.

It was a house full of loving details. Mom was creative in how she made it uniquely our own. She wouldn't hesitate to whip out her paintbrush or sewing machine to get a project done, and everything had a place so it could be easily tidied. It wasn't a huge house, but every space worked for what we needed (or at least that is what I remember as a young girl!).

When I was about eight, we moved to a bigger home leaving our cocoon for a totally different part of the city. I missed my neighborhood friends and teachers at my old school. One of my friends likened it to moving across the country, and after I moved, we would have sleepovers at each other's houses, making sure to bring our bikes and a massive bag of belongings for the big trip across the city. I missed that house, but over time, as I settled into our new neighborhood, I thought about it less and less.

Now that I am grown and have owned homes of my own, I am realizing how significant the influence of that first house was for me. I gravitate toward spaces that are on the smaller side. Each room in my home serves multiple purposes and can evolve as needed. I love homes that feel collected over time and reflect the lives and personalities of those who inhabit them. I like to be able to feel the presence of everyone in the house and find comfort in knowing that all my chicks are tucked into the nest even when we aren't in the same room.

I love spaces that are colorful, yet calm, with art on the walls that tells a story or evokes a feeling when I look at it. I love natural light and big leafy trees, which meant that when we were looking for our current home, our search was narrowed to a mature neighborhood and a house that let light in throughout the day.

Maybe what I remember about that first house is nothing like what it actually was. I do know that I grew up in a cozy home full of love and I wanted to create that kind of home for my family. It's a feeling that has stuck with me over years.

footprints.

→ *What do you remember about your first house?*
→ *How has it influenced how you live today?*
→ *Is your current home similar or different to your childhood home?*

MY TEN-YEAR-OLD EYES

I attended a retreat where we were asked to bring a picture of ourselves when we were about ten years old. My mom had a bunch of old photo albums, and I came across one of me sitting on the front steps of our house. My hands are folded across my chest, and I am leaning in, smiling *sarah hepburn.*

directly at the camera. I remember loving the striped dress I was wearing. It had a little tie that wrapped around the waist, and I would wear it to church and to Sunday dinner in the spring months before it got too hot. My dark hair frames my toothy smile.

The girl in the picture was so sure of herself. She was curious. She was creative. She was a dreamer. She was shy but confident. And her eyes—it was her eyes that stopped me in my tracks. Her eyes were bright. When I looked at her shining, dark brown eyes in the photo, I saw a girl who was fresh and hopeful. A girl who was confident and sure of herself. A girl who was ready to take on the world. I almost didn't recognize that girl as me. But there I was.

I brought this photo to the retreat. I wasn't sure what we were to do with it. Perhaps the act of finding an old photo and staring at it was the exercise. If that was the case, it worked. I hadn't stopped thinking about the photo since I tucked it in my notebook to carry with me. But there was more. We went one step further and wrote a letter to that person in the photo. I felt kind of silly at first. Whatever would I say to ten-year-old me? As I sat down to start the letter, I caught a glimpse of myself in the mirror in the room I was writing. I stared at my face, at the lines and wrinkles that revealed a life lived.

What I noticed most were my eyes. They looked tired. They looked worn out by life. Where, I wondered, was the twinkle, the excitement? I thought about the struggles in recent years with my health, always wondering when the next thing would happen. I thought about the struggles with one of my boys in school. I thought about the arguments with my husband. I realized that life had piled up and beaten me down so much

I had forgotten how to feel alive. I had forgotten how to be excited about life. I had forgotten how to be like the ten-year-old me in the picture.

I started writing the letter. And the words flowed fast.

Keep smiling. Life will throw you curveballs. Know that you can always choose how you react. You can always choose to smile. You can always choose to let your eyes shine. Life will get hard at times, but remember that even in the darkness, there is always light. But—and this is a big but—you need to practice smiling. Even when it seems super hard, you need to smile. Work those muscles. Get those endorphins flowing. There is something to smile about in every situation, no matter how dire it seems. Let your smile shine through.

That moment set me on a path to finding my smile. To finding the twinkle in my eyes. It was hard. At first, when I smiled, my cheeks would hurt and my muscles wouldn't know what to do. I smiled at everyone I could. In the grocery store. At stoplights. With my kids. I committed to finding something to smile about several times a day. Even when it really wasn't something to smile about I wanted to find the little nugget that would carry me through. I knew that if I practiced smiling, eventually the joy would find me. Even writing about smiling is bringing a smile to my face!

I still carry that photo of ten-year-old Sarah in my journal. I look at her every morning. I talk to her. I told her that I was carrying on what she had started all those years ago. I told her that I was recapturing her smile. Finding the twinkle in her eye again. Getting to know that girl who was so confident and hopeful.

Somewhere along the line, I had lost my confidence. Lost my twinkle. My eyes had dulled. I had stopped believing in myself.

No. More.

Seeing ten-year-old Sarah unlocked something that had been lying dormant in the midforties version of Sarah. I now carry both the ten-year-old Sarah picture and a picture of forty-six-year-old Sarah hiking in the mountains. That forty-six-year-old has a twinkle in her eyes and a big smile on her face. She dug deep and found those pieces of herself that she had buried all those years ago. They were still there. They had never left. I just needed a reminder to go looking.

footprints.

- *Have you looked at a photo of yourself from when you were around ten?*
- *What did you see?*
- *What would you tell your ten-year-old self?*

YOU HAVE EVERYTHING YOU NEED RIGHT NOW

Every morning, I sit down and write in my journal a few things I am grateful for. I have done this for years, but there's a shift now, a knowing that I am not taking things for granted that is making my entries have a deeper meaning for me. Things like gratitude for a hard conversation with one of my boys because not everyone has the privilege of having a dialogue like that with their child. Or gratitude for the quiet mornings and getting up even when it is freezing cold and dark outside. Looking back, I often express gratitude for clean sheets. Damn . . . I love the feeling of clean sheets!

When I write these entries, I feel it all in my deepest being. The simplest of pleasures or the hardest of things I am grateful for because they are all happening for a reason in my life.

With gratitude for what is and for the gifts that surround me, I have been able to focus on what is possible instead of what I lack. When I think about what I have been able to accomplish with my writing habits or the consistency I have demonstrated in my fitness practice, I am incredibly grateful for the focus, the people I have asked for help from along the way, and the things I have said no to so I could keep going.

Things that were once important to me have fallen away now. I am less bothered now if I don't get invited to an event. I have no urge to stay up late drinking because it impacts how I feel the next day too much. I have come to understand that I don't want to be around people who are envious of what I am doing in my life. I am careful with what energy I surround myself with. Phrases like "I am so jealous" or "I wish that could be me" drive me bonkers. When I hear that I think "But that *can* be you!"

More and more, I am content to be just me. I don't need anyone's approval. I don't need to do things I am not comfortable with, don't want to, or will make me feel like shit. It sounds cold and empty, but I don't push myself like that anymore. The ten-year-old girl knew that she had everything she needed. Somehow that knowing, that confidence to be herself, that drive got squashed over time as she moved through life. It has taken many years to untangle those feelings, to find my voice, to let go of what doesn't serve me.

I didn't always believe that I had exactly what I needed in life. I didn't always believe that I could choose how I responded. I used to look at families who skied together every weekend and wished that could be us. I used to be so frustrated that my husband worked all the time and was resentful of his job. I used to hate how it never felt like I had time for myself, even though I never figured out a way to carve that out. I used to think I always had to be the last at the party to be liked by others. So many feelings. All grounded in a feeling of scarcity and lacking.

I have always lived an abundant life. Even when things seemed really hard, there was always abundance to be found. **I just needed to remind myself that life happens *for* me. Not *to* me.** Each day is different, and I always have exactly what I need on any given day.

Gratitude. Abundance. Love. Light.

footprints.

→ *Take a moment to pause and write down three things you are grateful for right now, in this moment.*

→ *Think to a time you have struggled and ask yourself how could you make things easy?*

→ *What one action will you take this week to make a shift?*

A SHAMEFUL CAREER PATH...
AT LEAST THAT'S WHAT I USED TO THINK

I was at an event one evening not so long ago and chatted with someone I didn't know well. He wasn't entirely unknown to me, but it was the first time we had met in person. He was a corporate banker-type and was very keen to know what I did for a living. I shared that I had worked for the same organization he was currently at when I first graduated from university. We spoke about common people we might know and the type of work I was doing.

He asked why I left, and I simply said that I wanted something different and had moved to work for a marketing agency for a period of time. I then shared that working in the agency world didn't work out, so

I started working for another financial institution but in an operations capacity. At this point, he paused and recapped our conversation: wealth management to marketing to operations?

"Yes," I said. I then proceeded to tell him that after my third child was born, I left my operations role, went back to school, and worked in the interior design field.

"Wow," he said. "That is quite a change."

"Yes and no," I told him. Many of the skills I had learned in my previous roles translated into the design world. I solved complex problems with creative solutions. I listened to clients' needs and created transformational experiences for their homes. And I had to manage the budgets and vendor relationships to get it all done.

"Interesting," he said. I could see him thinking as I drew parallels in all the career paths I'd walked over the years. "So, what is next?" he asked.

"A book!" I proclaimed enthusiastically (as in, the book you are reading right now!).

"Oh, wow!" He wasn't expecting that answer.

I smiled and proceeded to share my evolving work as an author, as a storyteller, and as someone who helps others unlock their own stories through the power of habit. In that moment, I felt empowered and emboldened to fully step into the work I was so passionate about.

Shortly after our exchange, we were joined by others in our conversation and the evening continued with small talk and cocktail-type banter.

On the car ride home, I could feel myself grinning from ear to ear. It had been a lovely evening for a good cause, but it was one of the first times that I had owned and boldly told someone I didn't know what I was doing and the impact I hoped to make in the world.

You see, for the longest time, I felt like a failure. I was ashamed. I felt like I wasn't able to find a job and a career path that lit me up. I felt like people thought that I just bounced from thing to thing. I felt like I needed to have a linear career path where I worked my way up the corporate ranks. That, to me, was success.

The thing is, I didn't know any different. The examples I had around me growing up were of people who started in one career and stayed on that path until they retired. Accountants, engineers, bankers, and healthcare workers. You got a degree and you worked in the field in which you were trained. There was no wiggle room for jumping from job to job and industry to industry. When I moved from investment banking to marketing to operations to design, I found lots of reasons to rationalize my moves, but the reality is I felt a deep sense of shame that my career path wasn't what I thought it should be.

As Brené Brown says, "Shame is the intensely painful feeling or experience of believing we are flawed and therefore unworthy of acceptance and belonging."

The only way to release shame is to reveal it. Be vulnerable with it. Stop hiding. It wasn't until my kids were in high school and thinking about what came next for them that I started to share more of my journey. The more I shared, the more I realized that it was important for them to know that you aren't a failure just because one job doesn't work out. Maybe it's not for you. Maybe you have grown as much as you can in that field and it is time to shift.

Bit by bit, I started to own my story. I started to realize that the more I talked, the more comfortable I was with how my career had unfolded. It wasn't a bold, public declaration. I just didn't hide or downplay what I had done, as I had in the past. In fact, I was proud of the journey I had taken and shared stories without censoring myself.

Thinking back to that cocktail conversation with the corporate banker, I was proud to share my journey. I was excited to talk about my writing and the impact I hoped to make. I didn't walk away feeling small like I had in the past. In sharing my story, I had released the shame that I'd carried for all these years about my career path.

footprints.

- Where are you hiding in life?
- Are there people you trust to share what you are working on?
- How can you challenge yourself to be vulnerable about something you are proud of?

MY OBITUARY

In recent years, I visited the ruins of an old church and graveyard. The entrance was down an old road surrounded by farmers' fields. I paused at the entrance—the plaque told me that the church was first built in 1779. I felt instantly calm. At peace. Quiet. As I walked the grounds, I stopped to read the tombstones. When were they born? How long did they live? I could feel the power of the lives that were laid to rest. I felt like I was walking through a history of the community. I started to reflect on my own life. What would my loved ones remember the most about me? What do I want to be remembered for? Have I lived life fully? Will I have regrets in the end? All these questions swirled in my head.

I have long been fascinated with the "Births and Deaths" section of the newspaper. I almost always read the obituaries. Morbid? Perhaps. But I love seeing generational patterns in names. I love seeing where people were born and where they lived when they passed. It also fascinates me the details that loved ones choose to share. Some obits read like a résumé: "Jack went to XYZ high school, where he was a star rower. He then went on to study law and spent forty years at ABC law firm, where he spearheaded the most excellent expensive project ever in the city's history..." blah-blah. Can you hear my sarcasm?

In a world where, in theory, we can be whatever we want to be, why, at the end of our lives, are we defined by who others think we are?

What do I want to be known for? What do I want my obituary to say? What conversations would my loved ones have around my gravesite?

During that visit I wrote my obituary sharing how I wanted to be remembered. It would be a forward-looking obituary knowing there are still things in life I want to do. It was an exercise that gave me clarity about the missing pieces and helped me focus and make decisions in life going forward.

Sarah's Obituary

Sarah Hepburn. Born October 1974. She was a beloved mother, daughter, wife, sister, and friend. She met Brad, the love of her life, at McMaster University . . . blah-blah-blah.

Screw this. Clearly, this is the type of obit Sarah would have rolled her eyes at and never wanted.

Here's the real deal:

Sarah often wondered what people would say about her when she was gone. She wanted to be remembered as the vibrant, loving, deeply feeling, intuitive, active, and multilayered person she was.

Sarah loved to explore in life, was curious, and constantly wanted to learn more.

Sarah loved to travel, but she was never one to sit on a beach. Sarah's idea of a holiday was hiking in the forest or skiing down a mountain.

Sarah expected the best in herself and was always pushing herself hard—too hard at times—and her body loved to remind her to slow down. She saw possibility in others when they couldn't see it in themselves, and she just knew when someone was open to being encouraged forward.

Sarah's greatest source of pride was the relationship she had built with her three boys. Never one to shy away from hard conversations, she built a mutual trust with them that was a strength throughout their lives (even in their teen years!).

Everyone who spent time with Sarah was gifted with her presence. Known for her unfailing trucker mouth and perpetually dirty mind, she was always up for a good giggle. Never one for large groups, she loved smaller group chats, and you'd never leave a conversation feeling like what you had to say wasn't important.

For a long time, Sarah didn't think what she had to say mattered. Somewhere along the way she found her voice and understood that the people who needed to hear her were listening all along.

footprints.

- → Take a moment to ask yourself how you want to be remembered at the end of your days.
- → What will people say about you?
- → What would you like people to say about you?
- → Write your own obituary.

WHAT DO YOU WANT?

I started asking myself what it was I wanted with some intensity when my older boys started high school. I worried they would graduate from high school, and I would be left wondering. It was like I was moving toward some kind of deadline. Yes, I still had another son who would be entering high school when they graduated, but somehow I was feeling like my world was opening up beyond the focus on raising humans that had consumed my life and identity for the past seventeen years.

Who do I want to be? Why did I wait to ask this question until my kids were older, you might ask? Yup, I wondered that too. The short answer is that I felt like I had been running ever since having kids, never stopping to consider where I was going. I was in a constant state of catching up. Trying to keep on top of things and feeling like life was a tale of one step forward, two steps back. I was so deep in the immediacy of raising kids that I had never allowed myself to pause and consider what would come next. Any thoughts about what I might want seemed sort of selfish to me.

It was big and hairy and scary to start thinking about what my life might look like when it wasn't centered around my kids. Me! I was still in there. Hello! Who even is this person? What questions should I ask myself? Where should I even start? Who was I to think that there was something more for me out there?

But I had this nagging feeling that I just couldn't shake. It was partly driven by fear of growing old and never reaching my full potential (always a perennial comment on my school report cards!) and partly driven by a curiosity for what else there was for me in life. What would Sarah 2.0 and Sarah 3.0 look like?!

Instinctively, I've always known that my identity would evolve over time. There is so much out there to discover, and I never wanted to be pigeonholed into being just one thing. I never saw myself as only Sarah the lawyer or Sarah the doctor or Sarah the engineer. (Nice effing examples!). In a way, it felt noncommittal. If something didn't work out, I hadn't failed. So, I jumped from job to job in constant motion. Always seeking; never satisfied. Instead of finding the answers, it only confused my sense of self and the ability to say out loud what I wanted.

If I am being totally honest, I wanted the safe route. I wanted the predictable ending. I didn't want to get hurt or to hurt others. I didn't want to take any risks. I pushed myself to just the edge but backed off before leaping. I didn't risk failing. I didn't have the courage or confidence to allow myself to be vulnerable and take a chance. It was easier to do what was expected of me without asking if it was actually what I wanted to be doing.

I have since discovered that it is never too late to change. It is never too late to put your hand up and say, "Whoa, not sure that is for me." In my early forties, I started to feel like I had drifted in life. I had been so focused on everyone around me that I wasn't sure who I was inside.

Who do I want to be? What do I want? Simple questions yet so hard to answer. I want to be a woman who lives a life that has meaning. A woman who has a deeply connected relationship with her family. I want to be a woman who believes in herself more than anyone and is not afraid to take a leap and try things that are scary and outside her comfort zone.

I want to travel more. I want to connect with like-minded people who lift me up. I want to create something that helps others find meaning and purpose in life. Most of all, I want others to know that it is never too late to start fresh and thrive!

I feel like I am just starting to shed my cocoon. The cocoon of expectations, the cocoon of fear of judgment, the cocoon of fear of failure.

I want to be the woman who writes a book and launches a new business. The woman who rises above her own fears and insecurities to step into the life of potential that is waiting for her. I don't want to hide anymore.

By sharing my own experiences and stories, I will take you through a journey of asking yourself what needs to happen for you to understand what you want. It all starts with asking yourself what is the change you seek. What is working in your life? What do you want to keep doing? What isn't working?

After you have more clarity, you can begin to ask yourself what it is you really want.

It's a process. One that doesn't happen overnight, but trust me when I tell you, it is worth it. **Starting with one small step at a time, walk toward what it is you want for yourself.**

footprints.

→ *Carve out some space for yourself: an hour's walk or a long drive, alone, with no podcasts, no music, no talking—just you and your thoughts.*

→ *Ask yourself what you want. No pressure. No judgment. Just curiosity. See what comes up.*

→ *If you can't think of anything, keep asking. The more you ask, the more you will start to unlock what is buried within.*

your identity

> "We are all born with an inner knowing about ourselves."
> –Sarah Hepburn

When people have been married for a long time there tends to be the "we" talk. The "royal we." *We* like to do this. *We* want this for our kids. *We* want our retirement to look like this. It is all *we, we, we*. Or at least that's how it often sounds when you're with other couples.

I often wonder at what point the individual blended into a couple and life was only thought of in terms of *we*.

I have long struggled with this. There is a presumption when you talk in terms of *we* that both parties are aligned. *We* is such a firm statement it feels like it leaves little room for nuance or personality. Is the focus so much on the *we* that the *I* in the relationship no longer matters? Nope. But sometimes it sure feels that way. I know my husband and I don't always agree on this topic. It's something we have discussed over the years. He loves the *we*, the *ours*, and the *us*. And I fight it. It feels uncomfortable to me. If I am only a *we*, what happened to the *me*? What happened to *me* as a person? Even though she is still there, sometimes it feels like she is drowning in coupledom.

I've seen this over the years with other couples, when one voice is more dominant than the other. On one occasion, my husband and I were out for dinner with another couple, and the man had a large personality. I had only met him a couple of times; he was very funny and never short of stories to share. Our conversation turned to where they would like to live when their kids were all out of the house. He wanted to go somewhere warm. The way he was speaking, it sounded like it was a done deal. They were moving. She commented that there were other things to think about. A voice of reason, it sort of sounded like, but I wasn't so sure. I sensed that there was more that wasn't being said.

This back-and-forth continued throughout dinner. It seemed typical of how they interacted. He would make bold statements; she would temper them. At times, it felt loving, but other times, there was an edge. As I observed their dynamic, the one question I wanted to ask her was, "What do you want?" We knew quite clearly what was on his mind, but what about her? We could hear her gently pushing back and sounding not so sure about where they'd retire or what they were going to do on their next holiday or what things looked like for their kids. But what did she want?

Had she even allowed herself to ask that question? Could the idea that the future where the kids weren't going to be the center of their world be causing the tension? Probably. It's a huge shift from family focused to empty nesters. As I sat there, I couldn't help but notice how their relationship seemed unbalanced. At least that was what I felt at that dinner. He knew what he wanted because he had always been thinking about it. In contrast, at some point along the way, she stopped thinking about herself and her dreams as the blur of life with young kids took over.

Is asking yourself what you want like a muscle that you need to continue to build and maintain? I believe so. If you stop thinking and dreaming about the future, your field of vision narrows, so you can only see what is immediately in front of you. **If you don't ask yourself what you want, and you don't think about your dreams regularly, life will just chug along.** You will find yourself wondering how you ended up where you did. Wondering about what might have happened if you had been more deliberate or firm at times. And feeling resentful to those you love the most for always "getting their way."

footprints.

- What do you want? Right now. Write it down. Dream big. It can be wildly far-fetched and unrealistic—it doesn't matter.
- Ask yourself the question today. Ask yourself tomorrow. Just keep asking.
- Start to get clear on what you want. Keep writing it down.

WHAT IS ON YOUR DREAM LIST?

When I was a kid, I remember that the common question people would ask is: "Do you know what you want to be when you grow up?" I would hear other kids proclaim: "I want to be a firefighter!"; "I want to be a doctor!"; "I want to be a princess!"; "I want to be a superhero!" There was always a level of enthusiasm as an innocent child that could never be matched as an adult.

I don't recall being able to boldly proclaim what I wanted to be when I grew up. I idolized Laura Ingalls from *Little House on the Prairie*, and for a long time, I wanted to be a pioneer. I loved organizing and rearranging my room and could see myself doing that when I grew up. But I really didn't know.

As I moved through school, I was encouraged to think in practical terms. The question of what to be when you grow up was replaced with the expectation that you would end up in a trade or profession that would provide a secure income and afford you a stable life. It was never explicitly said, but it was implied that there was a limit on dreaming. Walls around what was and wasn't possible.

In my twenties, I bounced from job to job, I was good at making sure I always had money to pay my rent, put gas in my car, buy groceries, and have fun. I was always comfortable but never strived for more than what I had. As I moved into my thirties and had babies, life became chaotic. With the chaos came a small voice that chirped at me every once in a while. Something was off. I was just too tired and overwhelmed to pause and listen.

Just before my fortieth birthday, I attended a conference. There were a few speakers I was familiar with in the marketing space and some fascinating speakers on the power of the mind to transform your thoughts. Then, just after lunch, a speaker stood on the stage. No notes. No slides. Just a dark stage with a single spotlight. She spoke about dreams. She asked a simple question: "What have you always dreamed of doing?"

People in the audience shouted out their answers. Others were enthusiastically nodding their heads. I sat frozen. My mind was totally blank. I couldn't think of one thing that I had always dreamed about doing. Get a good job, get married, have a house, live debt free? Raise kids who were kind and didn't end up in jail? There is nothing wrong with any of that, but in that moment, I knew that all those things were what other people had told me I should dream about. I had never stood on my own to think about what it was I dreamed of doing.

Dreaming takes practice. I have had to learn to give myself permission to think about something that seems impossible or unrealistic. Comments such as "How are you going to pay for that?" or "There's no time for that" drive me mental. Dreams don't have limits. Dreams aren't something that can be put in a box. Dreams aren't something that come true for other people. Dreams are possible for me. Dreams are possible for everyone.

I have dreamed of taking a sabbatical in France or Italy or Spain. I have dreamed of hiking in the Himalayas and climbing Mount Kilimanjaro. I dreamed of traveling with my kids and my husband. I dream of dancing with my boys at their weddings and holding my grandbabies. I dream of a house in the country perched on a hill overlooking the water. A place where I can swim in the summer, ski in the winter, and hike year-round. I dream of being fit and fierce and active into my nineties. I dream of creating a community of like-minded people who want the best out of the relationships that are the most important to them.

Dreams don't come with a price tag or a timeline. Dreams don't have a project plan or a map of how they are going to happen. **Dreams are something that if you keep thinking about them and focus on what is possible, you will find that you start to move in the direction you want.**

Make a dream list. Write it down. Say it out loud. Think about it every day. But whatever you do, don't ever set limits on your dreams!

footprints.

→ *Write down five things that you've always dreamed about.*
→ *Now, write those five things down as if they have already happened. Example: "I lived in France for three months." When you start to bring the future closer, you make your dreams seem less abstract.*
→ *Notice the nudges once you write things down. What small steps can you take to make your dream a reality?*

NOTICE WHAT YOU NOTICE

I have done yoga off and on for years. When pandemic-land started, yoga happened at home away from the cozy studio I had been attending.

At home, I was able to take a deep breath as the instructor softly cued my next move through the magic of YouTube. There are many things about in-person classes I missed, but it turns out that yoga was better by myself, sometimes in my pajamas, in the quiet of my bedroom. I was able to really focus on me, without the distractions of others nearby.

A refrain I've heard from yoga instructors over the years is "Notice what you notice."

Each time they would say those words, I never knew what I should be noticing. Was it the way the twenty-something crop-topped girl next to me was bending backward into the position? Or was it the woman my age who let out a wisp of a fart as she settled into downward dog? Was it the faint sound of people talking in the other studio while I was supposed to be in Zen-mode? It was like the minute someone told me to "notice what I noticed" I was noticing everything around me except what was going on in my own mind and body.

The reality is that I have never been fully comfortable in a room full of other yogis. Attempting to breathe deeply while contorting myself into a sideways, backward position that I felt wholly unprepared for while having a side-by-side comparison of a young bendy type or listening to a sonic farter made it really hard to concentrate.

Notice what you notice.

Notice the spaces where I feel off balance? Maybe that's it. Maybe that is what I am meant to notice. I am not meant to be fully comfortable. I am not meant to be fully confident. I am not meant to be fully healthy. I am not meant to be fully in control.

Maybe life, like a yoga pose, is best lived on the edge. Pushing yourself past the point where you are comfortable, past the point where you are fully confident, and bending into an off-kilter position is where the sweet spot is. Where the magic happens.

I needed to retreat to the comfort of my bedroom to focus on what a yoga practice meant to me. I needed to retreat to be able to notice how I was feeling. Be able to breathe into each pose. Be able to hold the position in a way that made sense to me. Patience. Practice. Privacy. By retreating to a quieter space, I was able to truly listen to my body.

Notice what you notice.

Listen. Pause. Observe. Be kind. Be loving.

Take the cue. Walk to the edge.

Just watch out for the farting middle-aged yogis in your next class.

footprints.

→ *Find a quiet space, put on soft music, and take ten deep, slow breaths in and out.*

→ *Pause.*

→ *What do you notice?*

→ *Take ten more slow breaths.*

→ *Observe.*

DISCONNECTING . . . IN IRELAND

For the longest time, I never really thought about what I wanted. When I was younger, I mostly did what I thought I should be doing. I went to university, started working, and married on a timeline that seemed to "make sense." I moved from job to job and launched myself into motherhood while starting a new business. I kept moving. If something felt off, I didn't pause long enough to ask myself what it might be. At the time, I'm not sure I wanted to know. It just seemed easier to keep living the way I was. *Why rock the boat?*

There were all sorts of signs I was ignoring that something needed to change. I might have been able to convince myself in my head, but my body started to betray me. I had health issues and random infections. I was bickering with my husband and annoyed with my family. I had constant stress about work and my out-of-shape body. I was partying every weekend. Instead of pausing, I just kept going.

Until I couldn't anymore.

It had been a dark winter, and I'd been feeling down since Christmas. Things were busy with the kids. The interior design work I was doing was okay, but it didn't excite me like it had in the past, and I found myself increasingly irritated with my colleagues and clients. My husband was working a lot. I was lonely. I thought I was lonely because my husband wasn't around and my friends were all busy with their own lives, but in reality, I was lonely with myself.

I would love to tell you that I had a movie moment where I was lying in a hospital bed and knew that from that point on things needed to change, but it wasn't that dramatic. It had been a rough few weeks. I didn't dare tell anyone how I was feeling or that I had been regularly in tears. I had always been able to pull myself out of my funks, and I just figured eventually things would get better.

I had been eyeing a retreat in rural Ireland with Philip McKernan. He is a deeply intuitive human who creates experiences for people who know there is more for them in life but aren't sure what and don't know how to move forward. He challenges you in ways you didn't think possible. The retreat promised seven days in Ireland, without my phone and with a group of people I had never met before. I knew that something in me had to change and I was done with small tweaks, so one dark April morning, I signed up. Turns out, that decision would change my life.

I arrived feeling insecure and doubting why I was there. One of the first things he asked us all to do was hand our phones in for the week to fully disconnect. So much of my life revolved around my phone that it was practically glued to my hand. It felt like I was losing an appendage. I kept trying to check the time. I could feel a phantom buzzing in my pocket. I wanted to know something and would reach for my phone to google the answer. I sort of thought I might just like to "check in" and make sure everything was okay at home. But nope. Wasn't happening.

I had gone to this retreat as I intuitively knew I needed space, but I wasn't exactly sure what it was I was looking for. Traveling to Ireland might seem extreme, but there was something about Philip's work and the power of the land that I was keen to explore.

When I first met the others, everyone else seemed to have it together. When he posed questions for us to reflect on and write about in our journals, I would sit and stare blankly at my notebook unable to summon anything to write, while the others seemed to easily jump right in reflecting with ease.

After a couple of days of not having any connectivity to the world back home, I could feel myself slowing down. I was fully engaged in the group conversations, my mind barely wandering. Then we hiked the wild west coast of Ireland to let it all soak in. When I was hiking, I could feel the wind on my face and the burn in my legs. I felt alive.

I knew disconnecting was probably a good thing, but I didn't realize just how powerful it would be to step away from the noise of everyday life to listen to my own thoughts. I had deep, uninterrupted conversations with the others in my group. I had time to sit and journal, and time to walk and allow everything to move through me.

As the week went on, I could feel myself starting to unravel and open. I felt calm. We would hike each day with the fresh air and sea views as our guide. It was energizing. After our walks, I would return to my journal pages and write and write and write.

Disconnecting gave me the space to find clarity and pause. I never would have been able to get to that space if I hadn't turned off the noise. At the end of the week, I plucked my phone out of the box where it had been stored. Looking at it, I wasn't so sure I wanted to turn it back on.

Eventually, I did, with the knowing that it wouldn't be the last time I disconnected from the world to check back in with myself.

I came home from that trip not having answered the question of what

I wanted, but I was ready to ask myself that question every day until I knew. I was ready to work the muscle and think each day about possibility and what I wanted my life to look like.

I learned many things after that trip. I learned what I needed.

Time and space

I needed the time away from my everyday life. I didn't know how much I needed time away until I got there. While a trip away for a week is not always practical, I promised myself to get away even for a few days three times a year. Sometimes, I take the train into the city for the day and just disappear. No agenda. No plans. I wander the streets, then take the train home again. Something about the movement on the train and walking for hours resets my mind. The time and space from everyday life fills me up.

Movement

I move my body for at least thirty minutes every day. Movement is truly medicine for me. I start my day stretching and always get my workout in before the busy of the day takes over. At first, it was hard to commit to. I found life got in the way. Now I crave my morning workouts. And I walk. Outside. Rain or shine. Hot or cold. Walking helps me think. During the pandemic, my husband and I started walking together every night, and it has been the best thing for our marriage. Our walks have been a way to stay connected even in the midst of a busy life.

Iteration

Be patient. Be kind to yourself. Asking hard questions about life, no matter how simple they may seem, rarely are answered at first. Keep asking. Keep refining.

Take the time. Go for the walks. And keep asking. The more you ask, the more clarity will come. I promise.

footprints.

→ *Do you know what you need to recharge?*
→ *How can you carve time and space away from everyday life for yourself?*
→ *What will you do with that time?*

INTUITION MATTERS

I have always had good instincts about people. When I meet someone and get to know them, even a little, I generally have a good sense. I can remember one of the best pieces of advice I was given as a new parent was to trust my gut. A mom who was a few years ahead of me in the parenting game shared that many people would offer their opinions, including friends, family, doctors, and people at the grocery store; but at the end of the day, if something didn't feel right with my kids, I should always listen to my intuition. Always trust my gut. This piece of wisdom has served me well as a mother.

At one point, I worked for a financial services company that was founded on and prided itself on its analytic strengths. The business had been built around being able to make data-based decisions that enabled them to take unique risks, which at the time, no other businesses were willing to take. I loved working there. Everyone was really smart. Really focused. It was a "work hard, play hard"-type of place.

Culture was an important company value, and hiring decisions were made using a peer interview process. The philosophy was that you could teach someone the technical aspects of the job, but if they weren't a good match for the culture, things would never work out. Participating in the recruiting process was one of the highlights of my time with this company. I met with new university grads, senior executives, and everyone in between. At the time, we were mostly hiring for data analyst-type positions, and I interviewed actuaries, math students, computer engineers, and recent MBA grads.

I specialized in the behavioral interview portion of the hiring process and, after some time, was responsible for interviewing candidates for senior positions. These were seasoned professionals, and my job was to assess how they would handle various situations and if they'd fit the company culture. Keep in mind, we were hiring people who spent a lot of their day coding data and staring at spreadsheets, and I was interested in how they would work with other people. What would they do with all the data they were analyzing? Could they make decisions that would impact a broader group of people and communicate those decisions in a way that made sense?

We utilized a standard scoring method to evaluate, but in reality, I was able to get a good sense of how things would go after the first question. Once all the interviews were completed, the panel would meet and collectively come to a hiring decision.

It was at this point my strong intuition would often clash with the analytical environment of the organization. I remember sitting in those meetings reviewing the results of candidate interviews, and there were a number of times when a candidate did really well on their case interview but was a mess when they talked to me. I would share examples with my peers and an assessment of why this individual wasn't a good fit. Sometimes my evaluation was considered, but often my voice wasn't heard. I was just the "fluffy side" of the interview. The check-the-box part. What I looked at was subjective. The data didn't lie (apparently).

There were times when I started to doubt my intuition. Saying something is off just because you feel it isn't particularly convincing—even though I knew I was right! I've never been the loudest in the room, and it got exhausting to have conversations with people who would regularly slap data in my face. The culture of the organization was so trained to focus on the numbers that the nuance would be often overlooked. Asking questions in the behavioral interview challenged the candidates to share the story behind what they were analyzing. They had to share how they would interact with other humans, not just the data.

We are all born with an inner knowing about ourselves. We are all born being able to observe the world around us and make decisions based on our own lived experience. Somewhere along the way, though, we convinced ourselves that our head is stronger than our heart. That we can think our way through life and that what our intuition and instincts are telling us doesn't matter. I observed this firsthand when I worked for that analytical company. My intuitive strength wasn't valued in that environment, which was one of the reasons I ended up leaving the company.

Trust your gut. Trust your instincts. Trust your intuition. It might not always provide a clear answer, but it sure as hell points you in the right direction.

footprints.

→ *Have you ever trusted your intuition, even when you were being told to do something different?*
→ *Is there a time you ignored what your gut was telling you?*
→ *What did you learn from this experience?*

GOOGLE MAPS DOESN'T KNOW EVERYTHING

Before Google Maps, there were actual maps. You know, the rectangular sheets of paper that folded up and fit nicely into the glovebox of your car. Well, that is if you could wrangle the giant paper back into its original shape (I have always been challenged to figure it out!). The folds never seemed to line up as neatly as they originally did.

My husband and I have taken many road trips together. He at the wheel and me happy in the passenger seat navigating our every turn. I would sit with the map spread out on my lap, folded in such a way that I could see the immediate direction we were going but would have to flip it over to see more as we got further along in our journey.

I've always had a good sense of direction and can usually figure out where we needed to go, even when the map didn't have enough detail to guide us. There were definitely wrong turns, missed exits, and sketchy treks down dead-end roads, but we always got to where we wanted to go. Maybe not on time, but we got there. All while traveling down roads we didn't expect along the way.

On one road trip, we were barreling along a random country road headed toward the highway when my husband spotted a farm stand with fresh produce. Perfect, we thought. We could use some fresh veggies at home. While stopped, we discovered little spice packets at the cash. They were made by a local vendor and we picked up a few to try. These have become our favorite way to add flavor to meats and veggies. I have ordered them time and again from this spice vendor, even giving them as gifts. I've liked them that much!

We never would have found this little farm if we had been following a precise map. I like to think that maps are meant to point us in the general direction of where we want to go, and it's our job to figure out the rest.

The always-on world of Waze and Google Maps has meant that paper maps have become almost obsolete. We get in our cars, type in our destination, then start driving mindlessly. The automated voice directs our every move, telling us the fastest way to get there. We don't have to think; we rarely get lost; we just drive the car. Maybe we are chatting with our passengers or are listening to a book or a podcast. Maybe we are rocking out to a badass driving playlist or are driving in silence, our minds an empty canvas.

When I think about how our navigational tools have shifted from paper maps to technology over the years, there seems to be a kind of complacency. We've gotten lazy about thinking about where we want to go and figuring out how to get there. We read all sorts of self-help books, listen to podcast after podcast, and go to conferences that promise to unlock our inner gifts, which is all great. But what is missing in all the information that is out there is our ability to listen to what we already know inside us. That is, which direction we want and need to go next.

We have been conditioned to look for external validation and guidance instead of relying on our own intuition.

Reading a map is a skill. Interpreting the information that is on the map is something that can be learned. Knowing how to shift the direction we go comes from our intuition that is already there—it just needs some encouragement to come out.

I worry that we are surrendering our ability to trust our intuition to know where to go next with our reliance on tech. After all, we never would have found our favorite spice packets if we'd been on the direct route home that day.

footprints.

→ *When was the last time you drove without using GPS?*
→ *Did you get lost or have an adventure?*
→ *How do you feel without directions or a map?*

DREAMING OUT LOUD

We were out for dinner one cold February night. Just my husband and me. At dinner, there was an ease of conversation. After the most recent pandemic-land lockdowns, we were grateful to be out again.

But that night, it was something more. It was easy and connected. Neither of us sat there with expectations of the other. We were just happy to be together, curious about what the other had to say. Listening. It was almost like we were dating again after having been together for almost thirty years. I had a moment of belly flutters as he sat reading the menu across from me. Is it possible to fall in love all over again with the person you have lived with for so long?

We began to chat about what our summer would look like. One of the big things we learned from previous years is that we need to make plans. The summer past had been a giant dud. It had been full of uncertainty with our kids' plans constantly changing and evolving. I had been feeling wrecked after months of lockdowns and online school, and it was one of those summers where we needed a place to go and decompress. By the time we knew when we could do something, everything was booked. The days had been long and hot, and we had both struggled. Once Labor Day came and the busyness of school routines returned, neither of us felt refreshed heading into fall.

Lesson learned: plan something. Even if we have to change our plans, we need something to look forward to. It doesn't have to be huge, but it needs to be something, and it needs to be on the calendar.

As we sat there enjoying each other's company, we started to talk about the upcoming summer. We both wanted to do something. To make a plan. We chatted through our kids' plans and timing and decided what would work for us. As we brainstormed, we both got excited and were off dreaming about what it would all look like.

The next day after our dinner, we were like giddy school kids. We had said out loud what we wanted to do, and the wheels were spinning in our heads. In that moment, we were excited for what was to come. We had felt the power of dreaming and making plans.

footprints.

- What is it you want that you have been afraid to say out loud?
- Why do you think you have been afraid to say what you want?
- Is there someone you can share with? Someone trusted you can say things to?

QUIETING THE DISTRACTED MIND

> **DISTRACTED, HEP?**
> - play music
> - go for a walk
> - do 5 sun salutations
> - set pomodoro timer
> - 20 min nap
> - do something else

I glanced up at the sticky note that was posted on the wall behind my laptop. *Distracted, Hep?* Ha, I thought. That's an understatement. Since I had sat down to write for what was intended to be a sixty-minute session, I had scrolled through Twitter, peed, gotten a snack, zoned out on Instagram, organized my purse, made a cup of tea, and folded a load of laundry. As I looked up to see my reminder sticky note, I was catching up on blog posts in my newsfeed.

The sixty-minute session I had planned was now gone. I sighed. If this was the first time something like this had happened I would be more inclined to let it go and pick things up again tomorrow. But this was hardly the first time I had planned a work session and got derailed.

It is hard to describe what my brain feels like when focus isn't coming to me. Maybe you feel this too? I'm pretty sure I am not alone here. The feeling is at the top front part of my head, kind of in my forehead but closer to my hairline. Things feel fuzzy. Like I am wading through sludge. I know where I want to go. I know what I want to do, but I'm stuck. Clarity of thought is lost. The harder I try to get going, the more I spin. After a while, my brain hurts, not like a headache but a throbbing feeling that leads to a dull ache. An ache of frustration. An ache of exhaustion. An ache of disappointing failure.

Mind wandering, Hep?

I look up again at the sticky note. Yup. It is, I mutter. I pause, my hands hovering over my keyboard. *What do I need in this moment to move forward?* I close my eyes. I take a deep breath. I pause again.

When I open my eyes after a few deep breaths, I look at the words on the sticky note. Gentle reminders to myself of tools that I know work to help get me back on track. Play music. Go for a walk. Take a twenty-minute power nap. Do five sun salutations. Set a timer. Do something else. These are all things that help me when the brain fuzzies start to kick in. Some days, it's easier to reset. Other days, it takes longer. What I do know is that on days when I am able to reset, I shine. The blocks in my mind clear out.

These are the tools that work for me. Try them out to see if any of them work for you.

Visual

For me, nudges and reminders need to be visual. It can be as simple as a sticky note posted at my desk. It could also be the wallpaper on my phone or a note on the fridge or the bathroom mirror. Keeping the reminder at eye level in a place where I can't miss it is key.

Play music

Find a playlist that works for you. I have a variety of playlists that I use to refocus myself. I listen to a Binaural Beats playlist that helps for deep focus. Sometimes, I listen to classical music; other times, it's a playlist similar to the one at my local coffee shop. For me, music works when it isn't something that I'm going to sing or jump around to. It also shouldn't make me feel so chill that I want to fall asleep. Whatever you listen to should help focus your mind and set the tone for the type of work session you are doing. Try playing music and see if it helps.

Go for a walk

Get off your phone and step away from your computer screen. Put on your shoes and walk around the block. Bonus points if you live and work where you can get into nature easily. Take some deep breaths and get walking.

Take a twenty-minute power nap

Huh? This sounds counterintuitive, but hear me out. When you lie down, close your eyes, and shut your brain down for a short nap, you are resetting your cognitive energy. You are giving your brain space to recharge. When I was in university, I would always start each study session with a nap. I'd put my head down on the table and shut down for twenty minutes. This quick reset would charge me forward and start my studying off on the right foot.

Do five sun salutations

Stand up. Breathe in. Raise your arms above your head. Breathe out. Lower your arms. You can bend over and do the rest of the classic yogi movement, but the point is to breathe. Take a deep inhale. Pause. Then exhale deeply. Repeat. It doesn't take much to wake your body up with gentle movement and some deep breaths, but it makes all the difference.

Use the Pomodoro technique

The Pomodoro technique is a timed pattern where you work in twenty-five-minute increments with a five-minute break in between. You can use the timer on your phone or computer to keep track. There are also free apps you can download as well. I use the timer on my watch, so I'm not tempted to scroll by picking up my phone. Working in twenty-five-minute segments allows you to commit to focusing for a relatively short period of time. When I am working on a Pomodoro, I can get down to work faster knowing that it will go by quickly. I have even started to think about how long things will take in terms of the number of Pomodoro breaks I completed in a day.

Do something else

It is okay to admit that perhaps what you wanted to focus on just isn't going to happen. Even if you're on a tight deadline, stepping away and doing something else for a short period of time can be enough to reset and enable you to move forward with what you set out to accomplish.

If, after going through all the things that help you manage your distractions, you still can't get down to work, be kind to yourself. It is what it is. Beating yourself up won't help you get down to work.

When something isn't working, it's important to ask yourself why. Did it work at one time, but now the habit and routine need to evolve? Having the clarity to understand why something isn't working is key. It is not always easy to ask hard questions, but it is a critical first step in finding clarity about what you want and what works for you.

footprints.

➤ *Have you ever used one of the techniques that I mentioned above?*

➤ *What worked for you?*

➤ *How do you regain your focus and keep on track when you have deep work to do?*

RUNNING AWAY FROM HOME

One day, when I was about ten years old, I snapped the latch closed on my little suitcase. The blue leather exterior was faded and worn. The white stitched border was dirty and gray after years of use. I don't know how the suitcase came to be mine, but I loved it. The lining inside was a silky material. I felt like I could pack my whole life away in that one little suitcase.

I don't know what had precipitated my urge to run away, but as I took one last look at my childhood bedroom, I was sure that everything I could possibly need was in my little blue suitcase. I knew that if I just stepped away, everything would be okay. I just needed to go. Now.

I quietly slipped down the stairs toward the front door. I made sure to skip the squeaky third step from the top so I wouldn't make a sound. My bare feet were light on the carpet as I paused before opening the door. I could hear the clatter of my mom in the kitchen, the dog barking at the back door, and one of my sisters chatting about something she learned in school. I slipped outside. Phew, I thought, no one noticed.

I put my shoes on, picked up my little suitcase, and started down the driveway to the sidewalk. As I got to the end of the path, I turned and looked back at the house. In dramatic ten-year-old fashion, I whispered, "I'm not sure when I will see you again, but I need to run away now." With one hand against my lips, I mouthed "I love you" to my family inside.

I walked down the street. My suitcase was kind of heavy. There was a misty rain in the air. Hmm, I thought. I hadn't planned for wet weather. I continued toward the corner. As I got further from the house, I realized that I didn't really have a plan. No destination. No place to go. I only knew that I wanted to leave.

I stopped at the corner and put my suitcase down. I sat on the curb. I had been so brave to pack all my worldly possessions and slip stealthily out of the house unnoticed. But now that I had broken free and was ready to fly, I felt grounded. I had no flight plan. Nowhere to go.

To go back home felt like a failure, like I couldn't cut it in the real world. Like I wasn't able to make it on my own. But maybe, just maybe, if I went home, I would be dry. And I could eat something. And if I was dry and not hungry then maybe I could think of a better plan for the next time I packed my little blue suitcase and left the house.

I was hungry. That much was true. The drizzly mist was not ideal. I sighed. I knew in my heart it wasn't going to work this time. I would need some more preparation so that I could survive on my own. After all, I was only ten.

I stood up from the curb, gripping the worn handle of my suitcase and turned back toward the house. As I got closer to the driveway, I looked up and saw my mom standing at the door. She smiled and asked how my trip was.

"How did you know I'd left?" I asked her.

"Call it mother's intuition," she said. She reached her hand out to me and welcomed me back home.

As much as we want to fly the nest, there is something about the comfort of coming home.

There have been many times since this childhood memory that I have wanted to run away from home. Often these urges come when life is overwhelming and chaotic. I need a break to reset. Taking the time away gives me the clarity to see what changes I need to make when I do go back.

Even if it is a short walk to the corner with my little blue suitcase.

footprints.

→ *When have you needed a break?*
→ *Did those feelings result in you getting away for a bit?*
→ *What have you done to create the space you have needed to reset?*

WHAT'S NEXT?

Once I started asking myself over and over again what I wanted to do and who I wanted to be in life, I started to have a clearer picture. It is a process that takes time and is something I actively work on every day. Time to listen to what the voice inside—a.k.a. my intuition—already knows. And time to build the confidence to say things out loud that previously I would have kept to myself for fear of judgment or hurting others.

As much as life can seem more complicated the older you get, what is important to me has become focus. The relationships with my husband and kids are everything to me. If I am not healthy in mind and body, I can't be the person I want to be with the people I love the most. Health is truly wealth.

Understanding what works and what doesn't has guided me forward. The answers won't come by just sitting and thinking. Taking action, one step at a time, is what has revealed the path for me. Consistent habits have allowed me to weather the invariable storms and find the stable footing necessary to keep going.

unlocking the power of habits

> "Habits that are thoughtful, intentional, and aligned with what you want in life will make a difference even when you feel like progress is slow."
>
> –Sarah Hepburn

In his book *Atomic Habits*, James Clear defines a habit as "a routine or behavior that is performed regularly—and in many cases, automatically." The words "regularly" and "automatically" are key. A habit is something that you do consistently and you don't have to think and plan each time you do the thing you do.

For example, I brush my teeth every morning. I don't have to remember to do it. I just do it when I am getting ready each day. I also binge on nachos and salsa from time to time. Again, I don't really think about it. I just chow down. Brushing my teeth is something I would consider a positive habit in my life and one that, over time, benefits my health. The nachos on the other hand . . . not such a positive habit. Over time, they add extra pounds to my midsection and extra dollars to my grocery bill. To manage the nacho situation, I try not to buy them. Problem solved. Otherwise, if they are in the house, they will get eaten.

Two different habits. One that has a positive effect on my life and the other, not so much. When you are thinking about habits, you are playing the long game. Lasting change doesn't happen overnight. Bingeing on nachos once isn't a big deal. Bingeing on them twice won't really matter either. But over time, enough bowls of the crunchy fried and baked Mexican delicacies will add up to unwanted pounds in awkward places (I'm looking at you, blue jeans).

The point is that you can leverage habits for positive change in your life. As Clear says, "With the same habits, you'll end up with the same results. But with better habits, anything is possible."

You just need to be willing to start simple, be consistent, and keep going.

HOW HABITS ARE BUILT AND HOW THEY KEEP GOING

Once I started to understand that the chaos in my brain and body was one of the main reasons why I unconsciously relied so heavily on habits as a way to manage daily life, I realized that putting daily activities on autopilot meant they would get done before I got distracted. Having tools to keep going has meant that I could do more without getting stuck.

Where habits at first were an instinctive coping mechanism, they are now tools I leverage to feel more satisfied and joyful each day. Sleep and exercise have been key to supporting my mind and body. I now know I can leverage the power of habit to make meaningful changes in a way that is sustainable. Having this aha moment has enabled me to move forward with intention.

HAVING CLARITY IS KEY

What does this all look like? Well, if something is to last, it all starts with a stable foundation.

For me, it has been about knowing who I am and understanding what I want. Without this clarity, any attempts at meaningful change would just be an exercise of guessing what comes next. Life is too short for guessing and wandering from one thing to the next!

Life can be a funny thing (and I don't mean ha ha!). Rarely is life linear moving from point A to point B. I had to learn how to be patient and let go of control. I had to get comfortable with not knowing all the details of how life would unfold and trust that I was moving in the direction I had pointed myself.

Change doesn't happen overnight, but my having the clarity to understand what direction I wanted to go allowed me to keep moving even when it felt like I was taking two steps forward and one step back. The promise I make to myself now is that each day I take at least one step forward. It could be a walk around the block when I miss my morning workout. It could be texting instead of calling my mom on days when I am short on time for a proper phone call. I am still connecting with her and know I will call the next day. It doesn't have to be big. But it has to happen. Just one wee step forward.

START SIMPLE AND BE CONSISTENT

The more complicated a new habit is to maintain, the quicker you will drop it. For example, say you want to consider yourself a fit person who runs. If you are new to running, you sign up for a 5 km race to train for instead of starting at a marathon distance. Or you start by putting on your shoes and doing a run-walk combination for fifteen minutes. Keep it simple to start. And importantly, be consistent. If you start with your fifteen-minute run-walk combination and you do that consistently for a month, I bet you will be able to run for fifteen whole minutes without stopping.

STAY ACCOUNTABLE

Keeping with the running example, if you want to run a 5 km race it helps to have a way to stay accountable for your training. It could be keeping a running log. Or sharing your progress on social media. Or you could join a running group to surround yourself with people who have similar goals to you. As the saying goes, you are the average of the five people you hang around most, and if you want to become a runner, one of the best ways to do it is to hang out with other runners.

Your goals are going to evolve as you do. If you are consistent in your running practice, you are going to be able to run faster and further and your goal might shift from running a 5 km race to a 10 km race. Or you might add swimming and biking and race in a triathlon. The cool thing about getting clear on what you want, in this case, to be a fit person, is that how you move toward what you want will evolve over time.

Here's the thing, though; you are human and life happens. You might get injured. Your child might be home sick from school and you can't get your run in. Adapt how you train. Miss one day of running but not two. Most importantly, be kind to yourself. Life will get in the way and that is okay. It is getting back on track that matters.

footprints.

→ *Think about actions you repeat daily. What helps you succeed each day? What doesn't?*

→ *Where have you had clarity about what is and isn't working in your life?*

→ *Did the clarity help bring about change?*

ROUTINES FOR ADHD

One of my boys was diagnosed with ADHD when he was in grade four. It was no surprise, really. I had been on a first-name basis with the school principal for quite some time. School was a challenge for my son, and he was a hurricane of activity at home.

It was a constant struggle to help keep him on track. We tried tools to help him focus and to minimize distractions. We also understood how important physical activity was for him. He was on medication. He had longer to complete tests and was permitted a study aid in class.

As we worked through everything together, I researched and learned as much as I could about ADHD. I started to see patterns that felt familiar. Patterns in behavior I could identify with. Things that I struggled with as an adult. Difficulty focusing on a conversation without starting down a new tangent. Puzzles were impossible. We both could be very convincing even when we were full of shit. And deadlines. Oh, deadlines, they were merely guidelines and rarely met. The work would get done but often with rushing and drama.

I've also struggled to get work completed throughout my life. There would be days when I would sit at my desk and literally nothing would get done. Renegotiating deadlines happened almost all the time. Often, I would rush and miss a detail, or I'd finish something but feel like I could have done better. This has been the norm for me throughout my life. The scramble has, at times, made me feel like a colossal failure. I often struggled to get started on work. And when I did get going, I struggled to keep going and finish what I said I would.

I knew something was different. At some points, I was determined to find out what; other times, I just felt defective and defeated. I'd always been able to put on a brave and smiling face, so no one knew the struggle I had internally. In high school, I rarely studied because I found school easy, but in university, I really started to flounder. How was it possible, I would ask myself, that I can know how smart I am, have all these ideas, have great conversations to get started, then walk away to actually sit down and get the work done, but I'd stare blankly at the screen and do nothing?

I had sought help from therapists over the years, but there was never a fit. When I brought things up with my family doctor, she didn't really understand what I was talking about and observed that I was probably dealing with some anxiety and depression. I mean, maybe, but that just seemed too simple. It felt like there was more. I didn't meet all the markers for anxiety or depression, and I was generally able to pull myself back from my dark periods. I just felt more frustrated, like no one heard or understood me.

I eventually connected with a therapist who specialized in ADHD. At first, I went to her as a parent of an ADHD child. But therapy is never about someone else, is it? The more sessions we had, the more it became clear to me that, like my son, I also had ADHD. Eventually, I was formally diagnosed, even though I didn't really need to be at that point. I just knew.

Working with my therapist has helped me understand that I relied so heavily on predictable habits and routines throughout my life as a way to manage the chaos in my brain. If I could set something on autopilot, it had a better chance of getting done before I got distracted.

Undiagnosed ADHD for most of my life has meant chaos in my work life, my relationships, and how I treated myself. Being diagnosed in my forties has had a profound effect on me. I am only now starting to understand what it all means.

My physical health has been another noisy storyline to navigate since I was a baby. The trifecta of being a lifelong severe asthmatic complete with pesky nut allergies and skin that revolts at the slightest irritation have meant that my body can be chaotic and unpredictable. Random infections. Admitted to the hospital for asthma another time. Tough recoveries from C-sections.

Life would be rolling along then, bam, my face would be inflamed and I'd get a rash. Just when I felt in the zone. Just when I was feeling super productive and achieving things I wanted, my body would rail against my efforts. At least that is how it felt. As much as I have made progress to minimize the infections and the random injuries, there continues to be an element of fear as I wonder what will break down next.

Chaos in my mind and chaos in my body. The only way I have known how to manage and calm the chaos was to be consistent with my daily habits, to feel like my days had structure. I suppose it was a form of control. For a long time, I didn't have the awareness or tools needed, and I couldn't control what was going on in my mind or with my body, so I sought structure in every other part of my life to cope. I just didn't understand why I was doing it.

footprints.

- → *Have you had episodes in your life when you felt like your mind or your body was rebelling?*
- → *Did you pause to understand why?*
- → *Looking back from school to work, have you learned anything about the way you deal with deadlines? Have you created your own coping strategies or implemented tools to help stay on track?*

THE QUIET OF FIRST DIPS

When I was in high school, I was a synchronized swimmer and we were in the pool by 6 a.m. For much of the season, it was dark and cold when I rose from my bed, grabbed my things, and drove to the pool. There weren't a lot of cars on the road at that time of day, and the highway had a sleepy feel of waking up.

I was never one of the first athletes to arrive at the pool, but I was never the last. It was a comfort seeing a few cars I recognized parked in the dimly lit lot. As I made my way into the building I moved through a mix of cold air from outside to the heat and humidity of the pool deck. It always took a minute for me to adjust to the air inside. It was never fresh. Sometimes stifling. But after years of early mornings, it was familiar and comforting.

We were all senior swimmers with the synchro club, and we knew the drill to start training sessions. The warm-up was pretty standard, and the rest of the workout was posted on the whiteboard that our coach wrote out each morning. We gathered our goggles and bathing caps. We tucked our nose clips into the side of our suits and placed our towels and training notebooks nearby. These habits had been formed over years of mornings at the pool. We had big goals as swimmers, but we also had the watchful eye of our coaches monitoring our every move ensuring we stayed on track.

I loved it when I was one of the first swimmers to dive into the water. I loved the feel of the cold water against my warm face. I loved how still and calm everything was. It was so quiet. Often, I would pause underwater after I dove in to feel the moment. Then I would emerge and start the workout.

In the frenetic world of competitive synchronized swimming, the quiet when I was underwater was always my favorite. I couldn't hear my teammates. I couldn't hear the hum of the fans and heating systems in the pool. I couldn't hear my coach's barking instructions. It was just me and the silence of the water.

I now understand how much I need silence in my life. I need to deaden the noise around me. Life often is loud and chaotic. **It is those quiet moments, those moments when I dive deep into the silent waters, that reset my energy and allow me to move forward.** In the silence, I can start to hear what is around me again. I guess, even as a teenager, I knew I needed to find ways to retreat. For a long time, I would ignore this knowing. I wouldn't be aware or understand just how much I needed the silence to reset.

Those first dips taught me a lot. Splash, whoosh, silence. Reset. Surface. Move forward.

footprints.

→ *Where have you found quiet?*
→ *Are you okay with silence?*
→ *What have you learned about yourself in those quiet moments?*

STRUCTURED BUT RUDDERLESS

My teen years were a story of opposites. I was super structured in my synchronized swimming world. Early mornings at the pool, specific goals, accountability to my team and my coaches, intense physical activity, and dreaming about what was possible. I had teammates around me constantly, and we were all supportive of each other as we trained and competed. When I walked on to the pool deck, I felt like I belonged. Like I was meant to be there.

In my other teenage world, at school, I drifted. I was generally well liked but didn't really have a group of friends to hang out with. If I got invited to places, it would be more as an afterthought and usually only if I had been standing there while the conversation was going on. I went to a downtown high school, and there really wasn't any student parking, but they had made an exception for me as I would come from the pool each morning. This meant that I was in a position to drive other girls home after school. At first, I liked it. I felt like I was included and I belonged with the group. But then I started to feel used. Like the girls only talked to me late in the day when they wanted a ride home from school.

Swimming occupied most of my life outside of school, which meant that I didn't have much connection with student life. I didn't go to my high school graduation, choosing instead to go to a competition in Rome. Rome would be my last synchro meet, as I had decided to move on from the sport and start fresh in university. Part of me wanted to have a "normal" university experience, and the other part of me felt like I would never make the national team like I had been dreaming of. So I stopped. University seemed like a good time to make the change.

It turns out I would struggle mightily without the discipline of an intense competitive sport in my life. Without my parents and coaches around all the time, I had no off switch. I barely slept. I partied all the time. I mostly went to class but didn't really put in any effort to do well. I had made decent grades in high school without trying and figured university would be much of the same . . . nope. I found myself in the same position socially that I had been in as a high school student. Friendly with many but never feeling like I belonged. Except in university, I could compensate for this by drinking and being the life of the party. I think I intuitively knew I needed people around me and people with common goals, but I didn't find that. I was rudderless.

As I look back on the dichotomy of my teen years I am struck by a few things:

The people I surrounded myself with when I was swimming wanted to see me succeed. They were excited when I had a good swim, and I loved cheering them on too.

The structure of swimming had kept me on track. I had to be somewhere at a certain time. I had coaches who I was accountable to. I had teammates who were counting on me.

I was physically active when I was swimming. Turns out I needed that daily, intense level of activity to help keep me focused. The less physically active I was after I stopped synchronized swimming, the more tired I became.

Funny thing, when I became an entrepreneur and started my design business after leaving the corporate world, I would continue to struggle when there wasn't structure to my days and coworkers to be accountable to. It would be a number of years before I identified the pattern and started to shift.

footprints.

→ *Have there been times in your life when you have needed people around you to stay motivated?*

→ *What do you do to create structure in your day?*

→ *What keeps you focused and on track?*

DRINKING FROM THE FIREHOSE

Anyone who has ever watched the force and volume that a firehose pushes out water has a good idea of how overwhelmed, soaked, and flat on the ground they would be if they tried to drink from it.

This is a good description of how I have felt when I have a number of different deadlines happening at the same time. I procrastinate. I get overwhelmed by the sheer volume of what there is to do. I don't know where to start. I freeze. I avoid. Then I get frustrated. Sometimes I cry. After I spend time feeling like my head is going to explode, I try to get down and get to work. Sometimes, it works out and I get everything done on time. Sometimes, I renegotiate the deadline or reschedule things to make it work. Sometimes, I complete something half-assed and deliver it. Often, I feel like shit because it was just too overwhelming.

This has been a pattern throughout my life. Curious. Wanting to know. Getting distracted. Saying yes to too many things at the same time. Feeling overwhelmed. Never feeling like I was able to complete something as well as I could have.

The consistent thread in all of this is overwhelm. In school, I always found it challenging to break down an assignment or the study plan for an exam into manageable steps. I would look at the expectations that were set out and my eyes would glaze over. I wouldn't know where to start. Even just getting to the point of making a plan stressed me out.

I would delay and delay and delay until finally, I couldn't delay anymore. By that point, I would be short on time to gather information, to study properly, and to just get the work done. No matter what I did, I could never get on top of things.

The firehose was going fast and furious, and I was squarely the target.

Eventually, things got better. By about fourth year of university, I knew that the minute something was assigned to me, the minimum I needed to do was make a plan. Before I did anything, I needed to look at what was required and piece it into smaller sections. I needed to estimate how long it would take me to do something and make a plan on when it was all happening. I learned to allow for a time buffer if things took longer than I'd planned.

At first, this planning process was painful. I would read other things. I would disappear down rabbit holes of completely irrelevant information. I would get snacks. I would go for walks. I napped. But I did eventually sit down and make a plan. And it made a huge difference!

When I started working this way, I started to understand and, more importantly, remember how it felt when I was able to get down to work without the dance of wondering where I was going to start. **Memory is a powerful tool if you can train yourself to know how you want to feel in different circumstances.** With a game plan in place, I knew that doing something, even if it was the smallest thing, on my list would help propel me forward.

footprints.

→ *When have there been times when you felt like you were drinking from a firehose?*
→ *What could you do to make a plan so things don't seem so overwhelming?*
→ *Are there simple habits you could implement from the start to help?*

THE POWER SUIT

I had worked at a pool as a lifeguard and swim instructor for a few summers and despite loving my time there, I felt like I should get a "real" job. You know, practical experience that might help me once I graduated from university.

At the time, a "real" job to me meant working in an office and sitting at a desk all day. I envisioned myself as a powerful executive walking with determination down the halls. I'd have a desk and my own phone, maybe sitting next to a window, and I would share laughs with my coworkers in the kitchenette as we ate our lunch each day.

I would be like Melanie Griffith in the movie *Working Girl* taking the subway to work wearing my running shoes for comfort, then changing into heels to go with my suit once I arrived. I'd have a skip in my step as I expertly navigated the crowded sidewalks and dodged cars while jaywalking across the street sprinting into work each day. I would have friends at work who would greet me enthusiastically as I walked the halls. And I was utterly brilliant and known as the go-to person for how to figure things out.

I could totally picture myself working in an office for life. As an inexperienced university student, it screamed: "I've made it." Ahh, naive Sarah.

The summer before my final year of university, I got a job as a summer student at a wealth management firm. The dress was late nineties formal office attire, and before I started my mom took me shopping for a suit. We tried on a few options and decided on a navy blue one. The skirt was shorter, as was the style at the time, with a longer jacket that was tailored so it grazed my hips ending just above the hemline of the skirt. We bought navy blue shoes that looked like a loafer but were styled with a chunkier heel. And tights. Mom knew how much I hated pantyhose, so we compromised and coordinated my suit with navy blue opaque stockings. We finished it all off with three different tops to wear under my blazer and I was ready to go.

I loved my suit. I felt confident and powerful in it. The heels made my legs feel longer and stronger, and I adopted a certain swagger each time I got dressed. This was success, baby!

After a few weeks of strutting in my power suit, the novelty started to wear off. On the outside, I had blisters from my new shoes. Inside, I was unsure. I questioned everything I said. I wanted to disappear into the back of the boardroom and hope desperately that I wouldn't be called on to speak during a meeting. I felt like an actor playing a part in a movie about an office worker. I wondered when I would start to feel truly confident.

I now know that confidence comes from within. You can strut around in all versions of the power suit, but that energy will only get you so far. You have to believe in yourself first.

footprints.

→ *When was a time you donned your own version of a power suit?*
→ *How did it feel?*
→ *Did it help you do what you wanted to do?*

TAMING TWINS WITH ROUTINE

My boys were never good sleepers at night. Some well-intended distant relative sent me a book about sleep training that I excitedly read in anticipation of the magic formula to get them to sleep. Instead, all that ended up happening was I felt like a failure and an exhausted new mom. I was desperate and listened to anyone with baby advice in those early months. Note to self: only take advice from someone who has half a clue what it is like to deal with two babies at the same time!

What my boys lacked in the nighttime sleep department, they more than made up for in their naps during the day. They were champion nappers and never fought sleep at nap time. In fact, some days, they would crawl or toddle down the hallway and stare at their cribs waiting for me to plop them in their bed, hand them a soother, and cover them up with their favorite blankie. They would then roll over and be out cold for at least two hours. Yes!

Once I emerged from the newborn haze, figuring out a solid daily routine with my boys is what got me through those early years. I think I instinctively knew that they would eventually sleep at night, but in the meantime, I relished the quiet of naptime. I knew some friends who weren't so strict about naps and their baby would nap in the car or stroller. I just couldn't do it. I desperately needed a break during the day, especially when I didn't get a full night of sleep.

I can remember driving home after a morning at the zoo and looking in my rearview mirror to see two little sets of eyes glazing over. Shit, I thought, they're starting to fall asleep. They never transferred well from the car to their cribs, and I knew that the key to happy toddlers was getting that nap in. I reached behind me and tickled their toes. I started singing songs at top volume. I handed them both snacks. All in a desperate attempt to keep them awake until we got home. As I drove across the city, the singing got louder and the toe tickling more aggressive. I'm pretty sure I was throwing Cheerios directly at them toward the end of the drive. I screeched into the driveway. Put the car in park and quickly pulled them out of their car seats. They were sort of floppy-tired at this point, but I made it inside and was able to tuck them into their cribs where they conked out.

That wasn't the first time or the last time I had to resort to some "keep baby awake" tactics, but they generally worked each time. Those naps kept me sane.

While my original motivation might have been self-preservation, I soon came to understand my boys also relied on the structure of routine. We all knew what to expect. We knew what was going on. We all seemed to know that the house was full of happy people when they were rested and I had time to myself.

It was the first time I understood how important habits have been all my life. I had fiercely protected naptime, so I could have a break. **It was one of the first times I had understood how intentionally crafted habits could be used to do what I want.**

footprints.

→ *Think back to a time in your life when you were so tired you could barely function. What did you do to manage?*

→ *Did you learn anything then that you still do now?*

→ *Are there habits or routines in your life (like your morning routine, your baby's naps, dedicated time with your partner) that you fiercely protect?*

THE EARLY BIRD GETS THE WORM... AND THE QUIET!

Before I had kids, I used to hit snooze on my alarm clock multiple times every morning. I waited until the last possible minute to bolt out of bed, then rushed to get ready, quickly scanning the newspaper and grabbing whatever I could for breakfast. When my kids were younger, they would loudly wake me up nice and early. I would head downstairs in a daze, mindlessly scroll my phone, and stand at the fridge wondering what we were going to eat.

Whether I was hitting snooze or being woken by my kids, I was reacting to the day before it had even started. I was fumbling along hoping the day would be a good one. Hoping luck was on my side. And I was often frustrated and wondered why the things I wanted to do and achieve didn't happen.

Contrast what I just described with what my mornings looked like when I was a competitive synchronized swimmer. As I described earlier, all through high school, I would wake at 5 a.m. so I could be on the pool deck ready to go for 5:45 a.m. There was no stumbling out of bed. There was no wondering what my day would look like. There was no hoping that things would happen if I just winged it. I started each day with a plan so I could achieve the things I wanted to.

My early mornings ended when I went to university and left the synchronized swimming world. Well, sort of. In my first year, I competed on the varsity swim team, but I wasn't a very serious athlete at that point and did everything to sabotage my results. I stayed up late. I ate like shit. I sort of studied. I had gone from a super structured world where I rose early and had accountability to my parents, coaches, teammates, and teachers to one where it was entirely up to me to find the motivation and self-discipline to thrive. In my new university world, where I had more time on my hands than I knew what to do with, I struggled to self-motivate. It was easier to stay up late, lounge in bed in the morning, and let the day just happen than to get up early and start my day with purpose.

When I started working after university, I continued to roll through the day hoping that it would be a good one. Hoping that the stars would align and everything would go smoothly. Hoping that somehow I would find the time to exercise, read, cook a great meal, call a friend, write an awesome proposal, or go for a walk with my husband. Hoping that my life would be great. **I have since learned that hope without a plan will always leave you wondering why the things you had hoped for never seem to materialize.** I was hoping for the best but instead reacting to what life handed me each day. I was bolting out of bed every morning, jolted into reality by either the alarm clock or my kids, and not being deliberate about what I wanted my day to look like.

I was tired. I felt like a spinning top. I needed to make a change, even though it seemed overwhelming to do so. It was at this point, right around my fortieth birthday, that I started to really think about how I wanted to feel and what I wanted my days to look like. I started to observe my habits and keep track of what was working and what wasn't. This awareness was key. For example, I had forgotten how much I thrived in the early hours of the day.

Waking up before everyone else gave me the uninterrupted time and space to think about the day and be intentional with how I wanted to feel. This was a game changer for me. By the time everyone in my house woke up I was ready for the day. Not hitting snooze each morning was a conscious decision and has not always been easy. Habits take practice. Habits take time. I was feeling so much better with just one change; I knew rising early was a habit worth keeping.

A morning routine doesn't have to be complicated, but it does have to be consistent. I have tinkered over the years with what I do when I wake each morning, but I continue to get up early no matter what. Having this time to myself keeps me grounded and clears my mind. This one shift has made me a better human. When I have risen early, I no longer hope that the day will be what I want it to be. I have a plan and am ready to go.

I am grateful to have gone back to my early morning roots even if it took a lot of years to get there. My favorite time each morning, especially in the spring and summer, is when the silence of the darkness recedes as the birds start to sing and greet the new day. Early mornings to myself energize me and breathe life into my mind and body.

footprints.

- → *Reflect on times in your life when you felt in charge of your day. What worked for you then?*
- → *What is one simple shift you can make to feel in charge of your day?*
- → *Test out this shift for a week or two. Is this something worth keeping?*

THE SNOOZE BUTTON

Maybe I will just take today off. Maybe I need a break. I'm so tired. I just don't want to. I've been dragging the past few days. I can feel the focus slipping. I feel pulled in different directions. I feel like my brain is drained. I stand in the kitchen and stare. I have the urge to mindlessly scroll my phone.

My alarm went off this morning, and I didn't want to get up. It felt like I had just gone to sleep. The sheets were cozy. I could feel my body tucked in against the mattress, my head sinking into my pillow. Snooze. Just one snooze. Just a little bit longer in bed. I lay there staring at the ceiling. With all my being, I didn't want to get up. But I also didn't want the alarm to go off again and slide into the cycle of hitting snooze a bunch of times. I wanted to meditate and stretch. I wanted to drink my tea in the quiet of the house. I wanted to write in my journal and get my word count in for the day. None of that would happen if I hit snooze over and over.

As I lay there feeling the warmth and comfort of my bed, I remembered how good I felt when I wrote each day. How I felt knowing that I was one step closer to putting words down on the page for my book. I remembered how good my body feels when I moved it in the morning and how the dark and quiet of the early mornings with my journal and my warm mug of tea allows me to ease into the day feeling firm in gratitude and what I want to do.

I remembered why I got up at 5 a.m. every day. I remembered what I wanted to accomplish. I remembered how I wanted to feel. I remembered who I wanted to help. Lying in bed and staring at the ceiling, I remembered all those things. I sat up. I stepped out of the warmth of the bed into the cold air of my bedroom. I turned off my alarm and pulled a sweatshirt over my head. I headed downstairs to boil the kettle and start my morning.

I really didn't want to. But at that moment, the things I wanted to do became more powerful than what I didn't want to do. One step at a time. I knew that I just needed to keep going and eventually the momentum and energy would build again. The power of remembering how I wanted to feel and what I wanted to accomplish was what got me going.

I didn't want to stay in bed a minute longer.

footprints.

- → *When has there been a time when you've run out of excuses to do what you promised yourself?*
- → *What made you do what you promised yourself?*
- → *When you haven't done what you promised yourself, how did you move forward the next day?*

WHAT'S IMPORTANT TO YOU?

I spent a lot of my life running from one thing to the next. When I was a teenager, my world was my competitive synchro team and school. As a teen, I was "Sarah, the synchro swimmer." Once I retired from the competitive synchro world, I wasn't sure who I was anymore. University student? Sure. But I had no idea what I wanted to do with my life after university.

At one point, I was considering law school. After all, I liked politics, loved my Canadian law courses, and would disappear for hours at the library deep in research and writing. Seems lawyerly, no? I decided to write the LSAT to get myself started. However, I didn't prepare for the exam and did miserably. I then talked myself out of law school by telling myself all the people in my undergrad program were annoying and I didn't want to be around annoying lawyers as a career.

Who makes decisions like that? Me. I did. That is how I rationalized a decision when I wasn't confident enough to say it just didn't feel right. Instead, I sabotaged myself by not preparing for the LSAT and found reasons not to move forward.

After university, life rolled along. I got a job. Left that job and went to work somewhere else. Left that one too. Nothing ever felt right, and I hated working for other people and dealing with, what I thought were, arbitrary rules. I did manage to stay working at a bank for a number of years, and while the money was good, it was a super stressful place to work. Along with my work life, I got married, we bought a house, then had three kids. My thirties were a blur of work, kids, house, and always having to be the last one standing at a party.

When you are constantly running, there is little time to pause and ask yourself hard questions. *Who am I?* At one corporate retreat, we were asked to write down five words to describe ourselves. I had no idea what to write. I just stared at the page. I felt like I was doing everything for everyone else and there was nothing left for me to even begin to entertain the question.

You know when you are on an airplane and you are told to put your oxygen mask on first and then help others? I get it now. Once I started to help myself in my midforties, I was a calmer, more present human. Pause. Retreat. Quiet the noise. The process, this awakening from within, forced hard conversations with myself to get clear on what I wanted. It has meant hard conversations with people around me. I know not everyone who I am close to understands. I've been told that I have changed. At first, that hurt. But the reality is I am the one who has to wake up and look at myself in the mirror. And I better like what I see.

Getting clear on who I am has meant that I am a better mom to my kids. I don't feel like I have to be something I am not. It has enabled deeper connection with my boys. No longer do I feel like there are things I "should" say as a mother. All topics are on the table. Sex, booze, drugs, vaping—you name it, I will talk about it. Having a strong sense of self has meant that I talk to my kids without judgment (mostly), even though there are times when things they do drive me bonkers. My approach has been that I would rather know even the ugly than pretend everything is hunky dory.

It is not easy. But now, as I am solidly in midlife, I am excited for what comes next. I know I have the tools, the energy, and the patience to navigate life in a way that feels true to who I am.

footprints.

→ Who are you? How would you introduce yourself to someone new?
→ Write down five things that are important to you right now.
→ Take a look at the pattern of your days . . . are you doing or spending time with what and who you say is important?

THE DOWNSIDE OF HABITS

If habits are a routine or behavior that are performed regularly, then it is important to be reminded that if you repeat the same thing day in and day out, you will see change. It just might not be the change you are seeking. **Habits that are thoughtful, intentional, and aligned with what you want in life will make a difference even when you feel like progress is slow.**

We are human, and what worked at one time might not work at another. Take bedtime routines with kids for example. When my kids were little, I was really strict about bedtime. They were happier little people when they were rested. Bedtime was consistent in our house, and they never fought going to bed. They just did it because that is what they knew. However, as the kids matured, bedtime started to become a struggle. They wanted to stay up later. They argued with me that none of their friends went to bed when they did. I, however, continued to push the same routine that we had been doing. Except it wasn't working anymore. It took me some time to understand and admit that the bedtime routine that had once been so solid for our family, no longer served us. The priority was still that everyone was getting enough sleep, but the actual go-to-sleep time needed to reflect the age of the kids, and the nightly routine needed to evolve with the age of our family. The habit needed to change to remain a positive one.

Some habits become so ingrained in our lives that we're unwilling to test them in case they actually break. Take my morning routine. I love the quiet of the early morning. In fact, I obsess over getting up before anyone else just so I can have some time to myself. When I rise early I meditate, I stretch, and I write. It has proven to be the most important way to set my day up for success. There have been times, though, when I have been so strict, so rigid with my morning routine that I have retreated from social interaction at night because it might impact my morning the next day. Things like going out for dinner with friends, even though it wouldn't be a late night, would mean that I wouldn't have the time to prepare at night for the next day. I have gotten stuck in this cycle and missed opportunities for connection with others because I lacked flexibility when it was needed.

The bottom line is that what you do every day will have an impact over time, and it is important to regularly assess if the habits you have still make sense. The workout you started when you were out of shape isn't the workout you will be doing when you are stronger. Habits will evolve. You will evolve! If what you are doing isn't propelling you forward, then it is time to reevaluate.

footprints.

- Can you think of habits in your life that have grown with you over time?
- Have you deliberately evolved your habits or were you forced to make changes?
- Have you noticed a daily habit that does not serve you? How can you adapt?

simplicity

> "Take imperfect action and start simple."
> –Sarah Hepburn

Once you have a better idea of what you want, you can get to work on establishing the building blocks that will move you in the direction you want to go. As humans, we love to complicate things: *Hey, I have this great idea, let's do this and this, and let's add more to it too.* Before we know it, it all just seems too overwhelming and we give up.

Start simple. If you start a habit, build the muscle memory first. You can layer in complexity as you go. No hike starts at the top of the mountain.

You start with one step at the bottom. Then you take another. You'll likely take some detours along the way, but you start with one small, simple step in the direction you want to go. **Take imperfect action and start simple.**

Sometimes it takes another perspective to help you make some simple shifts. A few years ago, when I was running my interior design business, I met with a new client to select colors for her main floor. As we went through various scenarios and discussed the pros and cons of different shades of white (yes, white comes in many forms!), she repeatedly apologized for the state of her house.

Working in the residential design field I had seen a lot of homes, and trust me when I tell you I have seen some, um, interesting things. Not this house, though. My client's home told me a story of a family who fully lived in their space. Dishes in the sink, laundry waiting to be folded, shoes tossed by the front door, random socks scattered throughout and the various piles of papers, books, and magazines waiting to be read or recycled.

On the surface that may sound like a messy home, and I can only assume that is what she was apologizing for, but when I see houses like hers, I see a home that is full of life. Homes aren't meant to be perfect or fully furnished. Homes are meant to evolve, live, and breathe with the people who walk their halls.

As we continued moving through the main floor, I noticed that there were various piles of laundry everywhere. A pile on the sofa. Another pile on a chair. A basket parked at the foot of the stairs to the second floor. Yes, she had called me to help select a color palette, but what I really wanted to understand was what was going on with the laundry situation in her house.

After we finalized colors, I asked her if I could ask a question totally unrelated to what she had called me about. She nodded, and I gently said, "I would love to know more about how you do laundry in the house."

She laughed. "You don't think the piles of clothes lying everywhere is a good idea?! Laundry is a disaster in our house."

I smiled and said, "Why don't you tell me more."

"Well, as you can see, our laundry room is basically a closet area in the front hall at the foot of the stairs. The kids stand at the top of the stairs and throw their dirty clothes in the general direction of the laundry area. After a load is run, the clean clothes will get piled on the sofa to be folded and put away. Annoyingly, it seems that often we can't tell what is clean and dirty, so clothes will get washed twice! Honestly, I hate laundry. It never seems to end, and we spend a lot of time fighting about it."

The irritation and frustration in her voice was clear. Laundry had become a beast that seemed like it could never be tamed. We talked through some options. Simple things like putting dirty laundry hampers in each bedroom to eliminate tossing the dirty clothes down the stairs. We talked about implementing a system where a wash load cannot go into the dryer until the clean clothes that were in the dryer had been folded.

Nothing we discussed was overly complicated, and I could sense her frustration lessening the more we chatted. That day, I left her with the paint recommendations and went on my way.

About two months later, she emailed me. She told me that the paint had turned out great. But what she really wanted to tell me was that she made changes to how she does laundry after our conversation. She said there are no longer piles of clothes lying around waiting to be folded. That alone was a huge win.

And she wanted to tell me that she didn't feel like she was yelling at her kids to clean up like she used to. It had truly made a world of difference. She hated all the yelling. It made her feel like a bad mother because she couldn't get her kids to help around the house.

Sometimes it takes another perspective to see some simple shifts you can make that have a huge impact on your daily life.

footprints.

- *Is there someone you can ask for a fresh pair of eyes on something that is bothering you?*
- *Are there small issues in your home that have taken on a life of their own?*
- *What is one small change you can make today? Is it moving a table over? Posting a schedule?*

START IMPERFECTLY

I need the right notebook before I can journal. I need the right pair of shoes before I can run. I need workout clothes before I can start yoga. I'm too busy at work to add anything new to my schedule. There is too much going on with our family to take time for myself. I can't possibly prepare nutritious meals every single night. It just seems too hard to even think about adding one more thing to my day.

All these thoughts (and more!) have gone through my head at various points. I want to write more, workout more, eat better, get more sleep . . . on and on and on. But I never know where to start, so I don't. Or I start and my efforts fizzle. Then I get mad at myself and revert back to running from one thing to another each day.

I would find every excuse in the book to explain why the thing I wanted to do didn't work. The kids needed me, work was busy, I was at a bunch of parties and too tired the next day to do anything. But the biggest challenge was that to do the thing that I wanted to do I would get frustrated easily and give up because it wasn't what I had envisioned. It wasn't perfect. I'd give up thinking maybe it wasn't meant to be.

Start. Stop. Start. Stop. Always the same thing. I would fall into this cycle of constantly starting, getting really excited about something, then crashing. Over and over. Followed by self-loathing for not being able to stay on track. Yep. That was a predictable outcome too.

The gym is a classic example for me. Throughout my working life, I have been a member of various gyms and mostly just paid rent each month. You know, the automatic payment that is impossible to cancel once it is set up? Yeah. That one. I rarely went. And even when I did, I would sort of half-ass things. It just never felt right. When my kids were all in school, I joined an all women's gym in our local community. I thought it would be a good way to meet people, and I liked that I wouldn't be sharing workout space with meathead weight lifters (sorry if you are a meathead weight lifter). I remember being super nervous when I went for the tour and signed up for the monthly plan. They had a deal on (of course!), and I was happy to save some money on my latest foray into the fitness world. When I showed up, there were mostly really fit women. Nothing jiggling in their lululemon pants, and many wore only their sports bra showing off their muscular arms and abs. Okay, I remember thinking, they are just further along than me. I will get there.

I started going to classes. Each class was about an hour, and by the time I drove to the gym, did the class, and drove home, it would be at least a two-hour activity. I liked the classes well enough, but I didn't find the community particularly welcoming as I had hoped. It reminded me of high school with little groups of women gathered around giggling like teenagers. They didn't exactly welcome a newcomer. As I had done in the past, I started to find excuses why the gym wasn't right for me. Too much time. Too cliquey. The classes were too hard. The instructors didn't know my name. On and on. I gave up. I dropped out of the gym. It wasn't what I had envisioned it to be.

I had taken action. But I expected things to be perfect. I had this vision of what going to the gym would mean. I thought I would get fit, make new friends, and the gym would become a major part of my life. When the reality didn't match my expectations, I just gave up exercising. *Why bother? If I can't get fit going to the gym, what is even the point?* All-or-nothing Sarah had come out to play, and she had now moved from the all-in phase to the nothing phase.

After a period of time, I returned to my objective of wanting to get in shape. But this time, I decided to just start. I would start by walking every night. My husband joined me, which made the habit easier to keep and the walk more enjoyable. Then I signed up for one Pilates class a week. One class a week was achievable, and I was committed to that time slot rather than trying to go to the gym every single day. Bonus points that it was a small group fitness studio and the instructor would actually know my name. I started. It wasn't pretty. Pilates was something I had never done before, but my back had been sore, and I was hoping the focus on my core would help. I sucked. But I kept going. I had already paid and was expected to show up. Committing to one class a week seemed to keep me going. I found myself looking forward to my nightly walks to clear my head before bed. I kept walking.

It wasn't perfect. It wasn't what I had envisioned for myself as a fit person, but it was better than doing nothing. I had started. I had taken imperfect action. In doing so, I was building the habit in a way where I started to see results. I could hold a plank longer than ten seconds in Pilates, for example. That was a huge win. Over time, I started to layer in more movement each day. And now, I can't imagine a day passing without moving my body for at least thirty minutes.

footprints.

- → *What is the one simple thing you can take action on right now? Write it down.*
- → *Put that one thing in your calendar as you would a meeting or a kid's activity. Commit to the time. Commit to yourself.*
- → *Is there someone with whom you could share what you are doing to help you stay on track?*

GET PHYSICAL

After my failed gym attempt and ultimately discovering that a smaller, more personal Pilates class was a better fit for me, I knew that I needed to work out more than one day a week. My body in my twenties might have been okay with occasional exercise, but my body in my forties was definitely not okay with that approach. I needed more.

I wanted to make meaningful, body-supporting exercise a part of my life. I had been upset that I had stopped my gym membership. I felt like a failure that I didn't keep going, then I got mad that it wasn't a more welcoming environment. Then I promised myself I would figure something else out. It was a period of time where my body and mind badly needed movement, but more than anything, I needed to be nice to myself first.

I was a ball of emotion all tied in with my mental and physical energy and feelings around my body shape and size.

I knew that I didn't want to join a gym. It was just too much time to go back and forth, and I didn't want to deal with the high school-like environment of the gym I'd tried. Instead, I set up a small exercise space in our home and started working out a few times a week. I wrote out a series of weight, HIIT (high-intensity interval training), and cardio workouts trying to mimic what I had done in the various group fitness classes I had attended over the years. I would blast loud music, and sometimes break into a little dance all by myself in the basement. My workouts were between thirty and forty-five minutes and bam, done. This worked. Mostly. It relied a lot on internal motivation to work hard, and some days, I will admit I totally mailed it in on my workouts. I checked the box that I had worked out for the day but didn't really break a sweat along the way.

I discovered that the mornings were the best time for me to get my exercise in. I didn't like working out after I'd eaten, and if I waited too long, the day would get away from me and my workout wouldn't happen.

I also discovered that I needed accountability to keep going. I needed a challenge of sorts. I had been following a fitness instructor on Instagram named Phil who was super high energy and led thirty-day fitness class challenges. I signed up, set up my iPad, and got started. He talked through the whole thing while sweating profusely, but there was something about his energy that had me hooked. He reminded us (I say us because he made me feel like I was part of a team somehow) that we just had to give our best and just showing up is a huge win. He reminded us that we won't always feel like working out, but we will never regret it after we did. And it was only thirty minutes. Thirty minutes of intense, energetic exercise, and I loved it.

Phil was exactly what I needed to kick my home workouts into high gear. Turns out Phil was also what I needed to build my morning workout habit to the point where I don't start my day unless I've completed my workout. Whether it is a Phil workout or another workout, moving my body for thirty minutes every morning is just something I do. It is a nonnegotiable part of my day. I don't think about whether or not I feel like it (because, spoiler, I don't always feel like working out), I just do it knowing that I will feel better afterward.

* I learned that it would take trial and error to figure out something that would work.
* I learned that what my body needed would evolve over time and that is okay.
* I learned that the mornings were ideal for me to get my workout in, otherwise the day would get started and my workout wouldn't happen.
* I learned that I needed accountability. Be it a once-a-week Pilates class, signing up for a challenge, or even marking down my workouts in my weekly planner, I needed something to keep me on track.
* I learned that it needed to be simple to get moving. If it required me to drive somewhere, get changed, then drive home and shower all before starting my day, I wouldn't do it.

- I learned that I wouldn't always feel like working out, but I would never regret it afterward.
- I learned that if I missed a workout one day, it was okay. I just never missed two days in a row.

Most of all I learned to be kinder to myself. I learned to love my body for what it could do and challenge it just a little bit more each day. I didn't beat myself up if things didn't go according to plan. I just restarted the next day. Now, thirty minutes of movement a day is a nonnegotiable in my life. That is just what I do.

footprints.

- *If you aren't doing so already, what can you do to move your body regularly?*
- *When you don't feel like exercising, how do you start moving?*
- *Is what you are doing workout-wise moving you closer to your goals? If so, great! If not, why not?*

BASKETS FOR THE WIN

As the kids got older and started school, I was gobsmacked at the amount of crap that came home with them. Papers, crafts, books, binders, pencils, lunch bags, shoes, winter clothing, hats, party invitations, notes from school . . . the list went on and on. At first, I had assigned everyone a hook in our mudroom to hang their backpacks up. This worked for a while. But then miscellaneous stuff crept out of the school bags and onto the counters and floors. It started to pile up. The kids didn't need to bring certain things back to school. Some of it they would need again, but some of it was garbage. There was no way that I was going to sort it every night. At one point, I wanted to just light a match to it all and make it go away.

Instead, I created a system where the kids had a spot that was large enough to dump their belongings into but not so large that it was a bottomless pit and took up unnecessary space. I bought three baskets and placed them strategically near the entry from the mudroom. The basket was large enough to hold a backpack and corral all the loose papers that invariably spilled out of their bags. Each kid had their own basket, and the instructions were simple: put your backpack in the basket every day when you come home. The only things they were to remove each day were their lunch bags and any permission slips that needed to be signed. The rest would be dealt with later.

It took about a week of daily reminders when they got home to build the habit of where to put their bags, but it stuck. They had a spot that was easy to put their bag down without worrying about zipping things up or items falling out on a hook in the mudroom, and I was able to see the surfaces in our house again. It was a win-win!

What worked about this system? It was simple. It only required one thing for the kids to remember: bag in basket. Everything else would be dealt with in due course, but on a day-to-day basis, the crap was corralled. No more yelling. No more losing things. Minimal chaos in the morning. A basket. Simple. Mess contained.

footprints.

- ➤ *Is there a pain point in your house that could be addressed with a simple addition like a basket to corral the clutter?*
- ➤ *Take a look around the entrance that is used every day. What do you see? Does everything have a place? If not, ask yourself why.*
- ➤ *Now, look at your kitchen; are there any piles of paper? How you could address this?*

GETTING BACK ON TRACK

After I handed in the first draft of this book, I headed off on vacation. I needed to recharge and knew that, even though I had just poured my heart onto the pages, the work in the editing and rewriting process was just beginning.

I returned from my holiday ready to go. Ready to write again. Ready to refine. Ready to edit. Or so I thought.

Having received preliminary, high-level feedback from the editorial team, I knew what I needed to do to start turning my 58,285-word first draft into a *New York Times* bestselling masterpiece (you hear that, Universe?!). I had been visualizing holding the finished book in my hands. I had all the tools in front of me to get started again.

Except, I was stuck.

I was desperate to start again but totally overwhelmed. All I could see was the mountain of work ahead of me. I was spinning my wheels. Every time I sat down to write, I would stare at the blink, blink, blink of my cursor in a mad combination of frustration and despair. Was I ever going to be able to get back on track?

Spoiler alert: Clearly since you are reading this book, I figured out a way to get the wheels back on the bus. With each step forward, with each word on the page, I could feel the momentum gaining.

So what did I do to get back on track? Unlike Dorothy in *The Wizard of Oz*, I did not close my eyes and click my heels three times. Can you imagine?! Even though clicking my heels to get started wasn't an option, there were some things I did that helped me reset, get back on track, and calm the overwhelm.

I tidied. I cleaned up my desk. I swept the floor. I organized the kitchen counters. It didn't take long, but my getting organized settled my mind just by calming the space around me.

I made a list. I took a pad of paper and dumped everything out of my brain. I didn't worry about putting things into categories. I just got it all out as if I was emptying the junk drawer. Often, when I do a brain dump, I find that either I don't have as much to do as I thought or I have a lot to do but seeing it written down makes it less overwhelming.

I moved my body. When I could feel myself starting to get stuck again I would get up and move around. A workout, a short walk, or dancing like a fool in the kitchen worked. Even just short bursts of movement changed my mood and calmed my mind.

I asked for help. I set up a meeting with my publisher to chat about the book. I met with one of the editors, and she helped me identify three simple things I could do to get started. I haven't always been good at asking for help, but I knew that I would continue to stall if I didn't seek out support.

I hit the reset button. To get back on track, I stepped away from the big, overwhelming book project and attacked smaller writing projects. After taking a break, I was able to come back to the book project with fresh eyes and energy.

I started small. When I handed in my rough draft at the start of the summer, I was writing with ease. A month later, I couldn't focus. So, to start, I set a goal of 250 words at a time. After a few consistent writing sessions, I found my writing muscle was getting strong again. I was in motion and it didn't seem as daunting.

As athlete and author Rich Roll says, "Mood follows action."

I know that I will only get the desired result if I am actively doing something about it.

It turned out that calming the space around me, making a list, moving my body, asking for help, hitting reset, and starting small are tools that work for me when I am feeling stuck and overwhelmed. There is always a way forward.

footprints.

→ *Take a minute to reflect on a time recently when you've felt overwhelmed. Write down how you felt. What was overwhelming?*

→ *What did you do to get back on track?*

→ *What can you do to minimize this kind of overwhelm going forward?*

CHECKING OFF THE LIST

I have always loved making lists. To-do lists, goal lists, packing lists, wish lists—you name it, and I have a list for it. As a little girl, I would meticulously write in my homework book my list of things that I needed to do. My notes were colorful, and I loved nothing more than highlighting and organizing my to-do list into categories.

The satisfaction from checking things off my to-do list that started as a young girl continues to this day. Sometimes, I would put an item on my to-do list that I had already done. When I was younger I would add "make bed" as a to-do list item even though I had already done it, and it was something I did every morning anyway!

Lists help me organize my thoughts. They help me keep track of things. They help me know what I have to do. And they help me remember. Once I have a list on the go, I can roll through getting things done, checking off items on my list. They help me stay accountable to myself by being able to see what needs to happen. This is especially important when planning my time and managing all things work, family, and life.

On days when I don't get through what I had planned to on my list, I get frustrated. A cloud hangs over my whole day. In the past few years, I have learned to focus my to-do list and prioritize what goes on it. I take a little time each Sunday or first thing Monday morning to plan out my week. I review what is scheduled on the calendar, what I need to get done both for work and in my personal life. And importantly, I identify my top priorities for the week. There are usually three things. This has helped me get clear on where I need to focus. I also use this opportunity to shift deadlines around or reschedule things if it looks like I have committed to too much during the week.

Once I have my list for the week, I break it down even further when I sit down each morning and review what I have committed to. Each day I commit to my "big three." These are three things that no matter what, I am going to complete. Let's take a look at what this looks like in action!

For example, this week, I have a proposal for a new client that I need to send out by Friday. In this proposal, I need to break down what the deliverables are that I am committing to, and I need to map out pricing for this proposal. To be able to complete these two items I need to do some research in the industry that my client works.

End of week: proposal. This means on Monday, I'll block two hours to research. Tuesday, I'll block an hour to break down the deliverables (I know this won't take me too long because I had taken detailed notes already during our discovery call). On Wednesday, I'll set aside an hour to plan pricing. I will also spend an hour following up on any research that can add more details to my proposal. Thursday, I will spend an hour reviewing and putting it all together. On Friday, I'll send out the finished proposal with fingers crossed that it will be accepted.

Previously, I would focus only on completing the finished proposal and would feel overwhelmed by everything that needed to be completed before then. I would also find myself scrambling at the last minute to get it done and ask for an extension or hand something in that wasn't fully complete. Submitting a new client proposal without fully completing my research ahead of time or properly thinking through pricing never ended well. I was frustrated because I didn't feel like I was being compensated enough for the work and there would undoubtedly be misunderstandings with the client as things wouldn't be clear.

When I make the list and define the priorities for the week, then further break those priorities down day by day, I am far more likely to stay on track and get done what I want to.

footprints.

→ *Are you a list maker too?*
→ *How do you use lists to stay on track?*
→ *Do you share your list (or specific items on your list) with others for additional help and accountability?*

WHAT ARE YOUR BIG THREE?

Sometimes we can make things more complicated than they need to be. We plan and we talk about what we want to do, and we make lists. Then overwhelm kicks in. When I am overwhelmed, I tend to freeze and do nothing of what I had planned. When I'm in this predicament, I've found it helpful to step back and evaluate everything that is on my list. I am generally pretty good at prioritizing at a higher level, but I struggle with the smaller items.

I already mentioned my love of identifying my big three priorities for the day. By focusing only on those things, it helps manage the paralysis that comes with being overwhelmed.

I've even seen the power of the big three work with my sons. One of my boys had been complaining that he was having a hard time getting down to work because he had so many things to do that he didn't know where to start and would get lost on TikTok instead. I asked him what he was planning on accomplishing that day and he rhymed off about twelve items. *Um, okay.* I asked him if that was everything he needed to do. He said yes. "So, it is like, your whole list?" I asked.

He paused and looked at the list he had created on his phone. He then looked at me blankly and shrugged.

"If you were to pick three items from that list, what would they be?" I asked.

He looked again at his phone and promptly listed three items.

"Okay, focus only on those three. If you get those three items done, you are golden. Anything else is a bonus."

He nodded and headed off.

When I checked back in with him later that afternoon, he proudly told me that he had knocked off all the things on his big three list. He said it felt freeing to only have three things to focus on. And he said that he felt the sense of accomplishment that comes with getting things done instead of getting down on himself for not doing anything.

footprints.

- → Look at your list of things to do. What are the big three items that you are going to focus on today?
- → Does it help when you're able to limit your focus to three priorities?
- → What has focusing on your big three items enabled in your life?

AN IDEAL MORNING

One cold Sunday in January, I had the perfect morning.

I had slept in (for me) until about 7:15 and rose feeling energized and rested. I did my morning meditation, stretched, drank a glorious warm mug of tea, wrote in my journal, finished my book, ate delicious eggs, then went for a hike in the local forest with my husband.

It was freezing, but we dressed for the weather. While the cold can be hard some days, the sunshine that accompanies cold weather is the best. As we walked on the trail, we chatted. Invariably as the steps moved forward, we covered many topics. The sun was bright. Our cheeks were red. I felt connected and energized. I wanted to bottle the moment up.

After our hike, I thought through all the things I had done that morning: from the stretching and meditation to the journaling and finishing my book, followed by a yummy meal and glorious hike. It had filled me up. It was literally the perfect morning for me. It grounded me. I was nourished in mind and body and felt ready to shine throughout the rest of the day.

How could I create the perfect morning more often in my daily life? Why did it have to be reserved for a random Sunday here and there?

Stretching, meditation, and journaling are now a staple in what I do each morning. The habits are so established that I don't know how to start my day any other way. Reading is inconsistent, and I definitely don't get out for a hike each day. So how could I take things to the next level?

Planning makes all the difference. As the saying goes: fail to plan, plan to fail. What I do the night before sets me up for success the next morning. Have my book handy. If getting out for a hike isn't possible, make sure I have my workout clothes close at hand and a workout planned, so I can move my body without excuse. It all adds up. It becomes an automatic habit. A consistent, grounding behavior.

Once my kids are older and my mornings are not as dominated by their schedules, I will have more flexibility to do the hike that I so crave each day. In the meantime, I can still move my body. Just because it isn't exactly perfect, I can still strive to feel the way I do after a hike outside. I can still get a sweat on and a smile on my face.

Habits aren't about precision; habits are about intention. If the intention is to move my body, then incorporating some type of physical activity is vital. The important part is knowing what an ideal morning looks like for you and aim for that every day.

But be kind to yourself; you won't always get it right. Your mornings might not always be the ideal that you strive for, and that is okay. You don't live in a controlled bubble. Pause. Smile. Rest.

And get up and walk forward again tomorrow.

footprints.

→ *What does your ideal morning look like?*
→ *When you've had a day where you feel like you are moving and grooving, what have you done?*
→ *How can you recreate that feeling more often?*

consistency

> "Judge each day not by the harvest you reap
> but by the seeds you plant."
>
> –William A. Ward

How are you going to keep your new habit going? Luck? Willpower? Ha, no way! Give some thought to when you are at your best. Do you like to exercise in the morning or in the evening? Exercise isn't just going to happen when you feel like it. You need to have a plan for when it is going to happen. This means scheduling the time like you would a meeting. This means being super specific about what you are going to do. For example, "I am going to put on my running shoes, ride the bike for thirty minutes, followed by ten minutes of abs at 6:30 a.m. just before I have to wake up the kids for school." The less you leave to chance, the more likely you are to be successful. Make a plan and commit to yourself just like you would a work event or an activity with your kids.

INTENTIONAL GRATITUDE EACH MORNING

I have always felt grateful for the many good things in my life. Phrases such as: "I am so grateful" and "I am so thankful" are things I say often. But until recent years, I'm not sure I ever really understood how powerful it is to truly feel grateful—like chest-burning, eyes-watering gratitude.

For me, my journal has been a sacred space to work through my thoughts and feelings. It's a safe place for me to vent without hurting anyone's feelings. Journals are a trusted friend who will always listen, never judge, and never offer advice. Working through my feelings in my journal has kept me from melting down and saved me from saying things out loud in times of raw emotion that would be hard to take back.

Over time, I noticed a pattern had started to creep into my morning journaling. It was a consistent venting of feelings. There was a negative tone. I would pour ink onto the pages complaining about anything and everything. I would disparage myself for getting sick or being out of shape and feeling stuck in life. On and on this pattern went. I often felt better after sharing my deepest, darkest thoughts, but what I noticed was that the more I wrote that way, the closer the negativity and darkness was to the surface.

I started to realize that I was reinforcing those dark thoughts by writing about them every day. It wasn't actually helping. I wasn't turning my mood around after writing in this manner. Nothing was changing except that I was consistently frustrated about life. This was an aha moment for me. While my journal had been a safe place for me to work through my emotions, when I only focused on what *wasn't* working for me, I could never see what *was*.

I decided to rethink my approach to my journal. What if I led with the emotion that I wanted to feel? What if I wrote about it to start my day? What if, instead of treating my journal as a confessional, I used it to train my mind into feeling how I want to feel? My journal would still serve as a place for me to work through my deepest, darkest feelings, but I would start each day focusing on all the good in my life and what I was grateful for. I would feel deeply the words of gratitude on the page.

So each morning, I now start by answering the prompt: Today I am grateful for . . .

Some days, I write about moments such as gratitude for a family dinner. Sometimes, I am grateful for clean sheets (because who doesn't like a freshly made bed?!). On cold nights, I am especially grateful for a warm, safe home. Sunrises. A smiling barista. A car ride with one of my boys. Laughter with friends. Once I started each day focusing on what I was grateful for instead of leading with what was bothering me, I could feel the shift.

I immediately smile as I write a few lines of grateful thoughts each morning. It usually sets the tone for my whole day. Focusing on the good around me has helped me let go of focusing on what might be wrong or different from what I expected. It has helped me be accepting of the people I love for who they are instead of wishing for them to be something else.

My journal is still a place for me to work though my feelings, but no longer do I start with what is bothering me. Some days, I will come back to my pages to vent or explore ideas, but I always lead with gratitude to start my day.

I have long known that gratitude is a powerful tool, but I don't think I really understood what that meant. For me, it has meant focused, eyes closed, hands on heart, deep feeling into your toes kind of gratitude. It has been transformational.

footprints.

→ *What are you going to be grateful for today?*
→ *Commit to a week of beginning each day with gratitude and see how it impacts your mood and perspective.*
→ *Write it down! The act of writing something down carries more weight than mere thoughts.*

WHEN THE DAY WAS TOTALLY ON

I had one of those days.

Not one of *those* days but one of THOSE days. You know, the kind of day when you feel like you are rocking it from start to finish? When everything just lines up, you are on time, the work just flows out of you, and you are smiling and laughing from start to finish. Yes, they do exist!

What made the day different from others? Why did I feel so ON? It started with waking up after a solid night's sleep. I wouldn't say it was an unusually good sleep, but it was average for me. I made my tea, drank my water, and did my morning meditation while stretching. Then I put my music on and wrote in my journal. Afterward, I wrote. I even got my full workout in before I had to get the kids going and get myself dressed and out the door. Honestly, for the most part, it wasn't a morning that was really any different from what I had been doing for the past I don't know how many months.

With one big exception: no phone.

I had noticed I had started to slip into a pattern of running through my morning routine on autopilot. I was going through the motions. My mind would wander during my meditation. I was up and down like a jack rabbit while I was trying to write. And my efforts to focus were broken up by scrolling through Instagram, reading the morning news, and thinking of my to-do list for the day.

That day, when I felt so ON, I had only picked up my phone to play my meditation and then to put soft music on to write. Otherwise, my phone sat face down where I couldn't see it. I didn't even check any messages until after I had finished my morning workout. By the time I left the house for my first meeting, I was hugely satisfied that I had completed everything I had set out to do that morning. The feeling carried me throughout the day. Starting my day this way meant that even during little pockets of time when I would typically mindlessly scroll, my phone wasn't the first thing that I reached for to occupy the time.

All it took was ignoring my damn phone.

Holy crap it is hard. Even as I sit and write these words, I can feel it beckoning. Even with my headphones in. My phone is put away where I can't see it, but all I can now think about is taking a peek to see what I missed during the night. I know that one peek will lead to half an hour of mind wandering followed by more time trying to get back on track. It's a vicious cycle, and before I know it, my morning quiet time will be up. The sun will have risen, the house will be awake, and I will have to join the world again. I will feel like I didn't accomplish anything in those precious early hours I covet and protect so deeply.

I've discovered that when I have a morning where I feel like I have been focused and productive, it sets me up for the entire day. The day when I felt so ON was a direct result of what I did in the first two and a half hours after I woke up.

So how do I keep the momentum going? How do I capture more of those ON days?

For starters, I continue to move the phone farther and farther away from me. While moving my phone is a good thing, it still relies on my willpower to make it happen. And I am human. Temptation will always loom large.

I have been tinkering with an app called Freedom that locks me out of distracting things like social media, email, the news, and text messages for certain periods. I am hoping that this backs me up on days when my discipline to not mindlessly scroll is low. There are other tools out there where you can actually lock your phone in a box that can only be opened at certain times.

I have also placed sticky note reminders in strategic locations to make me pause before I start the scroll. A sticky note in my journal that greets me each morning and shares a gentle reminder of how good I feel when I am on track. A sticky note on the screen of my iPad where I write each day with a similar message. The first few times I giggled when I read the messages. They seemed so juvenile, yet they have been effective as a little nudge.

I also know that I'm human and not every day will be ON. That is okay. I have set a rule for myself that I can let things slide occasionally because distractions will happen, but I don't let them happen two days in a row. If I have a day when I am distracted and don't run through everything in the morning that I set out to do, I get back on track the next day. Giving myself this grace has meant that I don't get into a cycle of consecutive days of distraction. I just start again the next day.

The more days I have when I feel ON, the more I remember what ON feels like. And let me tell you, it feels damn good.

footprints.

→ *How do you manage your tech distractions?*
→ *If this is a challenge, list three ways you could make lasting change.*
→ *When you have had a day where you have felt ON, what has contributed?*

HABITS HELP, BUT YOU STILL NEED TO DO THE WORK

Habits make things easier; that's just a fact. When you set a behavior on autopilot, it frees you up to do and think about more complex things. It lays the foundation for you to take steps toward your goals. A habit is a tool, though, not a result. Think of a habit like a hallway. It enables you to get from one place to the next, but—and this is a big but—habits don't just happen. You need to do the work. Every day, you have a decision to make about what you are going to do, about the type of person you are going to be. Once a habit is fully established, this decision point each day becomes easier, but it still exists.

When I was in my midforties, I made the decision that I wanted to be a writer. I had always loved writing, but life got in the way, so I wrote sporadically here and there, mostly in my journals. I still thought of myself as a talented writer, though, with one exception—I wasn't writing! *Was I really a writer if I wasn't putting pen to paper?* Not really. You can't think the words onto the page. Are you a runner if you don't run? No. Are you a musician if you don't make music? No.

Visualization is a powerful tool, don't get me wrong, but **visualization without action is just an idea in your head.**

Let's get back to my writing example. I already thought of myself as a writer. That's a good thing! Identifying who I wanted to be was the critical first step. Now, I just needed to take action and do the work. So, one day, I sat down at my computer to write. Blink, blink, blink went the cursor. I typed a couple of words. Blink, blink, blink. It just kept blinking. I stared at the screen. How could I possibly be a writer if I couldn't put words down and if I didn't know what to write about?! I slammed my computer shut and walked away. *What was I even thinking?!*

I came back to it the next day. The pull to realize the vision I had for myself was now greater than the frustration of not knowing what to write about. When I sat down that day to write, I realized that I had decided that this was something I was going to do. It might be messy, imperfect action, but any movement toward realizing the vision I had for myself was better than no action at all. I didn't set a writing goal that day. I merely committed to opening a fresh note in my Evernote files and writing for twenty minutes first thing in the morning. That day, I wrote about why I wanted to write. I wrote about how I had always seen myself as a writer and that I was now putting my vision for myself into action.

I still didn't really know what I was writing about but thought that if I just started getting words down on the page, eventually it would all make sense. I sure wasn't going to figure it out standing still. You can't see what is around the corner from down the street. You need to walk toward the corner so you can see around it. I told myself that I would write every day.

I started by writing about what I knew: me and my life. I wrote about my childhood, about my feelings as a teenager, and what it was like going into university. I wrote about my experiences as a mother of three boys, including twins, and moving to a new town. I wrote about leaving my full-time job where I had felt successful and valued (even if I was stressed and not sure I liked it). I kept things simple at first. Importantly, I was consistent. I just kept writing.

At this stage, I wrote only for myself. I never intended for anyone to see what I was writing about. I was like that person who is so out of shape at the gym that they go when no one is there so they can quietly work up their strength. I had decided to write. I was taking action—quiet action, but action—over and over.

The more I wrote, the more I learned about my writing style, things I liked to write about, and when I was at my best writing. I learned that I did my best, most focused work in the early hours of the morning before the sun was up, before the house was awake, and before the noise of the day had started. I learned that I liked writing on my iPad instead of my computer because it wasn't as easy to toggle between screens and get distracted. It was a smaller screen, which somehow helped my focus in those dark, early morning hours.

I had decided to write. I was taking action. I was learning as I went. I repeated. I did the work. I kept going.

It wasn't easy. I learned that to rock my morning writing sessions, I needed to get a good night's sleep. I learned that my morning writing sessions actually started the night before in how I prepared for the next day. This was the harder part to maintain, but despite lots of ups and downs, I kept going.

The biggest thing I have learned is that if you aren't clear on why you are doing something, it becomes really easy to stop doing the thing you said you want to do. **Your why needs to be bigger than your excuse not to do it.** For me, I knew that if I didn't pursue writing, I would wake up later in life with regret. Regret at not taking that first step to get words down on the page. Regret at giving up when things seemed hard. Regret at not taking action and trying to move things forward.

Habits can make things easy, but at the end of the day you still need to do the work. You still need to understand why you are doing the thing. You still need to take action. You still need to learn from it. You still need to repeat the habit over and over while refining as you go.

Writing, for me, was just something that I knew I needed to do. That was my why. I knew that I couldn't live with myself if I didn't at least try to make it happen. You wouldn't be reading the pages in this book if I didn't take that first step.

footprints.

→ *What is a goal you would like to achieve? Why is that your goal?*
→ *What is your why? Why do you do the thing you do?*
→ *What is the one thing you can do to take consistent action to move closer to your goal?*

BRICK BY BRICK

I stood there on a steaming hot July day marveling at the pace the bricklayers were moving. The crew had started early to beat the heat, and they were already around one side of the first floor. Their skilled hands moved at lightning speed. Slap went the concrete, plop as the new brick landed on top, scrape went the trowel smoothing the bits that weren't needed. Slap, plop, scrape. Slap, plop, scrape. Brick by brick.

There was chatter among the crew. They had music playing. There was the rattling noise of the cement mixer grinding up the concrete to be laid on top of each brick. Everyone had a job, and they knew what to do. Their process was cemented and hardened by habit (ha, see what I did there?).

I couldn't stop watching: the pace, the skill, the cadence, the consistency. It was mesmerizing.

It made me think about the saying "brick by brick" or "step by step." It sounds cliché, but it's true. You don't build a brick wall at once. You start with one brick, then add another. And to build a wall that is stable and can withstand nature requires skill to know what will work best. Skill and time. Trial and error. Learning by doing.

For me, figuring out what habits work is like building a brick wall. Maybe that's why I was so fascinated by the bricklayers that summer morning. You start with one simple brick. Then you layer in something to help it stick. Then you add another brick. You build the foundation and structure so that it stays and withstands the impact of outside forces.

Growing up, I was always a voracious reader. I read all the time: in the car, at night, during class, even walking to school. I always had a book in my hand. A few years ago, I had stopped reading. My phone was always close by, and I would get sucked into reading the news or mindlessly scrolling through Instagram. I had a stack of books on my bedside table, but they would sit untouched night after night.

I was pretty overwhelmed at the idea of reading a whole book. That seemed daunting, like I would never finish it. But I knew I wanted to start. So I cleaned up the space. The leaning tower of books was organized, sorted, relocated, and um, dusted. Once I had a space that was calmer and less chaotic, I promised myself that I would start by reading one page a night. Just one page. But before even cracking the spine of the book, I needed to deal with the phone issue. I decided that just like the bricklayer would put on their hard hat as they walked onto the construction site, I would put my phone in "do not disturb" mode, plug it in, and set it aside as I walked into my bedroom each night. And just like the bricklayer had the materials needed to lay bricks already at the construction site, I had already chosen what I was going to read.

I started. I walked into my bedroom, switched my phone to do not disturb, and plugged it in. I opened my chosen book and read one page. Reading one page quickly progressed to more, and the habit has mostly stuck. It's just what I do. At a minimum, I read one page a night. The key to building this habit was that I identified what I wanted to do, then set myself up for success by creating a space that would help me.

Brick by brick. One page at a time. **Habits don't happen just because you want them to. Setting up your environment to work for you makes all the difference.**

footprints.

Identify what you want to do more of. Example: I want to read more.
Identify where. Example: I want to read more at night before I go to sleep.

- *Clear out distractions. Example: Take a moment to sort and organize my bedside table to create a calm space for reading. Turn phone to do not disturb, plug it in, and set aside.*
- *Start small. Example: Read one page a night.*
- *Acknowledge your success. Example: I have read at least one page each night for the past four nights. Last night I even read ten pages!*

SLIPUPS AND STUMBLES

It had been a week of indulging: snacks, sugar, late nights, booze, little sleep.

I had been working diligently on optimizing my daily routine. Focusing on sleep and movement was giving me a ton of energy. But then we went out on Saturday night. I ate the kitchen sink in pub food (man, those sweet potato fries and onion rings were yummy!). I had some adult beverages. And I stayed up late. My body clock woke me up at my usual time in the morning even though I felt like I had barely gone to sleep! I rose Sunday morning with a blinding headache and didn't feel like doing much of anything.

Enter a nap, a walk outside in the woods, grocery shopping, and some sorting for the week ahead. The nap was key. I could not have moved forward with much of anything without that damn nap! But then it wasn't just a Sunday, it was Super Bowl Sunday. So I had more junk food and more booze. The off switch that I had been working so diligently to train had left the building. After the game and after cleaning up, I finally headed to bed. I was tired but wide awake.

Now, it was Monday morning. The alarm went off. I lay there contemplating getting out of bed. It was freezing outside, and the cold air felt like it was seeping into every corner of our house. I got up. I drank my tea. I meditated. I wrote in my journal. And I attempted to do my morning writing. The kids got up. Everyone was out the door for the day. And my workout loomed. I did not want to move. I was so tired from the weekend, and my body felt gross from all the crap I'd filled it with. I started by putting my gym clothes on. Then I folded laundry and washed dishes. The house was soon clean, and I was out of excuses not to work out at this point.

I started my program, but it all just felt irritating. I didn't want to be there at all, but the session was only thirty minutes. That's it! Surely, I could get through a half an hour. But after twenty minutes, I was ready to throw in the towel. Screw this, I thought. My legs feel like lead. I can barely raise my arms above my head, and the round of burpees I just did made me want to lie on the mat in the fetal position and cry. Then something started to shift. With five minutes left, I could feel a glimmer of energy return to my body. I wasn't jumping up and down, but I didn't feel like a zombie anymore either.

The workout ended, and I put my equipment away. I smiled. I was so glad that I had pushed myself to do something that I knew in the end would make me feel better. I just had to get myself to start. After all, isn't that what it's about? Just starting? If you only just start something you are in a far better position than if you never started at all. Get yourself to the start line. Put the gym clothes on. Just start.

footprints.

- → What have you done when you didn't want to do the very thing you said you wanted to do?
- → What did you do to get back on track?
- → Did this awareness change your actions going forward?

THE POWER OF JOURNALING

I've spoken about keeping a journal, and I've had one since I was a little girl. It has been a place to chronicle life and work through my feelings. I never worry that my words won't come out as intended or that I will offend anyone. It is a safe space to dream out loud, share feelings of joy, speak my fears, and rant when I am pissed off. My journal has been a cheerleader, a therapist, a best friend, a coach, and a keeper of all secrets. It never has opinions, is never critical, is never mean, and I can say what I want to it without worry.

Over the years, my journal of choice has evolved. As a young girl, I liked the fancy journals complete with locks and fluffy feathery-headed pens (remember those?!). Now I use a simple Moleskine notebook or a sketchbook with blank pages. I have kept most of my journals—I am not sure why. They aren't meant for anyone but me, and I rarely go back and read them. Yet my ink-stained notebooks mark the passage of time. A story of what goes on inside my head. A life lived, a chronicle of dreams and emotions captured.

Just as the type of book I write in has evolved so, too, has my journaling style. Now, I use it as more of a mindset tool than a diary of teenage angst. At times, I have followed a structured approach where I use daily prompts such as listing five things I am grateful for and what I will do to make today great. In the past, this method has helped to focus my journaling and establish my headspace for the day. Other times, my approach has been more freestyle, and I write about whatever comes to mind that morning.

Currently, I blend some structure with some freestyle. I always start by writing down a bullet-point list of what I am grateful for. I conclude by writing what I want for the future as if it has already happened. The middle of my journal practice is pretty unstructured, and I write what is on my heart and my mind at the moment.

My notes of gratitude each morning can be as significant as being grateful for a warm, safe home, or as simple as being grateful that someone else brought the recycling bins up from the curb. Some days, I write a super long list and other days only a few items. In recent years, I have found that the deliberate act of writing down what I am grateful for has allowed me consider what is good about life even when things seem bleak.

For example, my journal helped me through our Christmas vacation one year. We had planned a fun family ski trip, but it went off the rails when a deer ran into our car en route. Then, three days later, my youngest son broke his leg on the hill. Nothing had gone as planned. I was exhausted. I was mad. Between ensuring my boy was comfortable after his break, figuring out rental vehicles, filing insurance claims, and a myriad of other logistics, I didn't want to do anything else.

For a hot minute I sat in my pity party for one, but then I cracked open my journal and started to write. As I listed all the things I was grateful for the negative crap faded into the background. No one had been hurt except the car from the deer incident (the deer ran off into the woods). My son's broken leg did not require surgery, and after the first few nights, his pain was not as bad. I had spent some amazing time on the ski hill with my older boys, and we were able to enjoy après ski drinks at the pub. We were all together as a family and had figured out a way home. Journaling helped me process my negative feelings and realize all the good that surrounded me. Even though our holiday looked nothing like what I thought it would, I was grateful for all the things it had been.

In the same manner that I write about what I am grateful for each day, I also list what I want to have happen in the future. This keeps my dreams and goals top of mind. I write them down as if they have already happened. The power of visualization makes them seem real. I can clearly picture the goal happening.

For me, journaling started when I was young as a way to explore how I was feeling and dream about the future. Now, while I still journal as a way of self-discovery, it's a habit that is as much a part of my day as showering. With each note of gratitude, I am constantly reminded of all that is good. As I write about what I want the future to look like, I find myself intentionally shaping the decisions I make each day in service of those goals.

I believe that everyone should take five minutes each day to put pen to paper. **Journaling has brought clarity, a sense of gratitude, and focus to my life.** Creating a space to remind myself of what is good, express my feelings in a safe place, and think about my goals has helped me to strive to be a better version of myself each and every day.

You don't need a fancy notebook. Any piece of paper and pen will do. If you don't already write daily in a journal, I encourage you to start. I promise you won't be disappointed.

footprints.

↠ *Do you write in a journal each day?*
↠ *If not, why don't you start tomorrow?*
↠ *Try it for a week and see how it makes you feel.*

STEADY HAND

Years ago, when I was going through a rough time with one of my boys, my dad offered me a simple piece of wisdom: "Keep a steady hand." At first I was annoyed and thought that there was no way it could possibly be that simple. Steady hand, my ass, I would think when we were speaking. I needed to do something. I needed action!

I keep coming back to that piece of advice over and over again. It has guided me as a parent. It has guided me as a business owner. It has guided me as I navigated health challenges. What does "keep a steady hand" mean? It means stay the course. It means no knee-jerk, impulsive decisions. It means trust that the situation will sort itself out over time and that you will know when to act and when not to.

Throughout my journey in understanding how to leverage habits for success, I have learned that if it feels like something isn't working to listen and observe before making a change. In other words, keep a steady hand. Maybe there are other things going on around me that are impacting what I do daily. For example, when I have had a series of late nights because of work commitments, it often means I am not able to get to bed as early as I usually would. For a couple of mornings, I would still rise early but would be tired throughout the day. Then I would have a morning when I slept longer and didn't get through my usual morning routine because of a later waking time. I started to wonder if maybe getting up so early wasn't working anymore, but I realized it was the impact of some late nights and catching up on sleep. With this awareness, I now give myself permission to rest when needed rather than make any radical changes to my morning routine.

Steady hand has been a guiding force as a parent, especially when parenting teenagers! It has shown me patience and reminded me to pause. Even when managing their planning "skills." Yes, "skills" is in quotation marks for a reason. If they tell me that they are doing something on the weekend with five days' notice, I mostly roll my eyes knowing that the plans will change ten times in between. I have learned to keep a steady hand, keep the lines of communication open, and wait and see what will happen before reacting.

Habits rely on a steady hand. Consistent, purposeful effort over time is when the juicy change will happen. Keep a steady hand.

footprints.

- *Think back to a time in your life when you realized it would have been better to pause.*
- *How could you have handled the situation differently?*
- *When you've paused, how did it feel? Did it help? Did the action you eventually took change from what you were initially going to do?*

accountability

"Alone we can do so little. Together we can do so much."
-Helen Keller

They say that most New Year's resolutions are done and dusted by the middle of January. There are varying stats on this, but the main point to take away is that New Year's resolutions get blown up pretty quickly! It doesn't have to be that way. For starters, stop trying to make big changes during the most hyped time of year. Don't wait until an arbitrary date—hit go today!

You don't have to do it alone. Tell someone what you are trying to do. It could be your spouse, your best friend, or your Instagram peeps. For example, if you are usually a coffee date kind of person, but you are trying to walk more, consider suggesting a walking date to catch up with a friend. I started doing this a few years ago and now it is almost a given that I will lace up my shoes and hit the trails with a friend to hang out instead of sitting on my butt at a coffee shop. Exercise and social time for the win!

Staying accountable to yourself is just as important. I keep track of my writing goals in my weekly agenda. At the end of each week, I total my word count. This has become a powerful tool for me to keep writing because I am motivated to not miss a day.

Trying to build new habits is really hard when the people around you don't have the same goals. I have struggled with this for years. I used to go to a party and plan to leave early so I could do a big hike the next day and not feel hungover. But I would get caught up in the rush of socializing, and before I knew it, I was stumbling home late and missing my hike in the morning. I tried not socializing, but that was hard and I missed people. Instead, I booked something the next morning that I couldn't change. Then I found a trusted friend at the party to hold me accountable if I looked like I was settling in for the night. This helped.

footprints.

→ *What are ways that you can hold yourself accountable for what you want to do?*
→ *If you need outside help, do you have the right community of people around you to keep you on track?*
→ *Does having someone to hold you to account help keep you on track?*

LISTENING TO THE WHISPERS

We moved to a new community when I was eight months pregnant with our third baby. It was a pretty chaotic time with three little kids. The first winter in our home was a blur of sleepless nights and struggling to keep my head above water. At times, I felt like I was drowning.

When my youngest turned one, I was invited to join a book club with other moms who had kids the same age. It turned out to be a bit of a rowdy group with books being the excuse to get together. Book club was a release for all of us from the tedium of parenting small children. It was an opportunity to make friends in my new community and pull me away from the isolation of small kids. To this day, some of the women I met in that book club are my closest friends.

The first night I attended, I walked over with my neighbor. We were both nervous to meet a new group of people and brought travel mugs with ciders, aka travelers, with us for the short walk. By the time we got there, I had downed two of them and was starting to feel a little buzzy. That set the tone for the night. Buzzy.

I immediately developed a reputation in the group for being always ready to party. Just like my early experiences drinking in high school, booze loosened me up. I was loud, lively, outgoing, and ready for anything.

I didn't always remember what I did or what I said each evening. One night I even lost my glasses. Embarrassingly, it turned out they had fallen behind my bedside table. I guess in my drunken state I had thrown them aside as I was getting into bed.

The first few years of this kind of partying were fun. They felt light, and we were all ready to blow off steam. However, as the years went on, I was remembering less and less of the night, my hangovers got worse (thank you, perimenopause!), and I would feel like shit for days after.

I tried to pull back on the drinking, but it never worked. It was like I didn't have an off switch. It was all or nothing Sarah again. There was never just one drink for me, despite my best intentions. I would say I was just having one drink and wasn't going to stay late; but once I started, I never wanted to stop. I actually started to avoid social events in an effort to avoid drinking. It felt lonely. I didn't like the focus on drinking but worried I wouldn't have any friends if I didn't partake.

I was more drawn to intimate gatherings where I could have deeper conversation and connection than drinking at large parties. I felt far better about myself than forgetting what I did at night and feeling like crap the next day. As I started down this path, I realized that the people I was closest to still wanted to hang out with me. They liked me for who I was not for how I partied.

footprints.

- → *Do you act differently when you meet new people to try to fit in?*
- → *How does it feel?*
- → *Think about a time when you felt most yourself. What were you doing? Who were you with? How can you feel this way more?*

LOSING MY WAY WITHOUT STRUCTURE

I had never failed a course. Ever. I had never even come close. I was by no means a top student, but I got decent grades. I didn't really try, but I showed up to class, absorbed what I heard from the teacher, and mostly handed things in on time. School was school. I was curious but not always about what I was being told I had to learn, and it wasn't unusual for me to have a book stashed under my desk to read when the lecture started to bore me. Exams were a challenge because I never did any work leading up to them, but fortunately, they were never worth enough marks to really impact my overall grades.

Mostly I floated through school. I showed up, did the work, sort of paid attention, and had teachers who would keep me on track. And with my busy swimming schedule, I had a limited time when I could do things anyway. My life, at that point, was pretty programmed, so I got done what I needed to in a limited time.

When I went to university, though, it was a whole new world. I was no longer swimming competitively. I was living away from home, and I was entirely responsible for my life. What I did, what I ate, what I drank, when I came home, when I woke up. Everything. I never had this kind of freedom before. I was so excited. No one was going to tell me what to do!

The first few weeks of university were a blur of parties and figuring out life on campus. I sorted out my classes and got my books. I attended the lectures, took notes, went to pub nights, and partied some more. Things seemed to settle into a rhythm at this point. Everyone was starting to focus more and more on school. I was too, sort of. But not really. I bombed my first test in I can't even remember what course. Shit, I remember thinking, that is not good. What made it worse was that I wasn't really sure how to catch up.

It wasn't unusual for me to have a nap during a lecture. They were always so long and boring and sitting still was hard for me. I would sit down to study and then read anything but what I was supposed to be studying. I made notes in preparation for tests but could never remember what I needed to know when I sat down to write the test. I had no idea what I was doing and no one to ask for help. Instead of doubling down on my classes, I found more parties. I scraped through school.

In high school, every minute of my day was accounted for, and everything I did was prescribed. I was accountable to my coaches for what I ate, how much I weighed, when I did schoolwork, when I had to show up at the pool, and the effort I had to give to swimming. Now, all of a sudden, in university, the only person I was accountable to was myself. And I had no fucking idea what I was doing.

I made attempts to recreate some of the structure I'd had around me in high school, which sort of helped. I tried to wake up at a regular time. I tried to make a study plan. I tried to go to the library to work instead of staying in my noisy dorm, but it was a struggle. By the time the first term ended, I arrived home a mess. I was exhausted, I had gained a ton of weight, and I was barely passing. For a girl who was used to doing well in school without trying and excelling in her sport while being constantly surrounded by her teammates and coaches, I felt like a lonely, colossal failure.

Until I didn't have it, I had no appreciation for just how much I needed structure in my life to thrive. At university, the onus was on me to create the structure I had thrived on in high school. I needed to be invested in what I was doing and motivated to get results. I headed off to university after high school without particularly considering what I wanted to get out of the experience.

Because I didn't have an end goal in mind, the first term of university turned into an exercise in letting loose and bottoming out.

footprints.

→ *Did you have a similar experience in university or living on your own for the first time?*
→ *Were you able to help yourself?*
→ *How can you find ways to feel a sense of accountability when you work on your own now?*

DANGLING THE CARROT

Sitting down to study was always hard for me in school. I could read books I was interested in all day but retaining information I wasn't particularly interested in was a colossal effort. My typical study sessions would involve me cleaning and reorganizing my room. And doodling mindlessly in my notebook. Usually a nap, too. Oh, and snacks. Always the snacks. It didn't seem to matter how much I planned or needed to do, it was always a Herculean effort to get started and keep going.

One year, toward the end of high school, I was struggling to stay on track during the final exam period. No amount of breaking down the tasks was helping. And my room was so clean it was like I lived in a museum.

I looked down at the notebook in front of me and read what I still had to review for the next day's exam. One item. I had only looked at one item in the past two hours of trying. I felt deflated. For sure I was going to fail. And I had three other exams that week.

I got up from my desk and went downstairs. Dejected, I plopped down in the kitchen where my mom stood making dinner. "I am going to pretty much fail every single exam this year," I said.

She paused as she chopped vegetables and commented, "That sounds a little dramatic."

But it wasn't. I felt so much pressure to do well at school. University was right around the corner and every mark mattered. How would I ever get into schools if I flunked all my exams? In that moment, I told my mom that I was just going to wing it and see how much I had retained from class. Studying was useless. I was just getting frustrated and diving down a big suckhole. Yeah, a suckhole! Did I mention I was in tears too?

Mom looked at me as I sat there wallowing in all my teenage girl drama and told me that exams were going to happen whether I wanted them to or not. Pretending they weren't happening wasn't an option. We talked about what would motivate me to study. We talked about taking more frequent breaks and moving around instead of trying to sit there. We talked about rewards and what I would look forward to once exams were over. Honestly, in that moment, the biggest reward I could think of was being done!

Then Mom pulled a giant carrot out of the fridge and waved it in my face. She said, "We need to dangle the proverbial carrot in front of you so you have something to motivate you to study."

Seeing Mom waving this carrot around the kitchen looked ridiculous, and we both started laughing. How would a carrot ever motivate me to study for exams?

Mom took me by the arm and marched me up to my room, carrot in hand. She surveyed my sparkling clean room and went to the bulletin board that was mounted above my desk. She took the carrot and hung it up on the bulletin board using a smorgasbord of pushpins to hold it in place.

"There," she said. "When you look at this carrot, you can smile remembering this conversation. And know that the time will pass sooner than you think." She encouraged me to use the carrot as a cue to remind myself to get back to work, and that good things come when you put the work in.

With that she went back downstairs, and I stared at the carrot and giggled. Then I sat down to work. The carrot didn't solve all my distraction challenges, but it did give me something to focus on other than the work at hand. And it reminded me that exams would be over in just a few days.

At the end of the week, when exams were over, the carrot was still mounted on the bulletin board above my desk. By then it was shriveled and soft and not very appealing, but it had worked. I had been able to get through the week with a giggle and a gentle reminder that I could do it.

I don't remember how I ended up doing on my exams that year; but what I do remember is how a simple thing like a carrot offered me hope as a reward for getting through a tough exam week.

footprints.

→ *What works for you as motivation when you are struggling?*
→ *Is there anything you use to focus on when you are having a hard time starting?*
→ *When you have been motivated to get something done, what is it you've been working on? How can you do more of that type of work?*

THE KITCHEN WHITEBOARD

Getting everyone in the house on the same page makes all the difference. One of the many parts of motherhood that I was unprepared for was being the gatekeeper of the family calendar. Kids' activities, school events, family events, school holidays . . . you name it, I was the central reservation system for it all. *Mom, what time is skating? Mom, when is our next school holiday? Mom, is it this weekend or next weekend that we are going to Nanny's for dinner? Mom, Mom, Mom, Mom!*

I needed a way to help the kids find the answer to their question without always coming to me. Like many homes, our kitchen has always been home base. When the kids were younger, they would often eat sitting on stools at the kitchen counter while I buzzed around on the other side.

The side of the fridge was directly in their line of sight, making it the perfect place to hang a whiteboard where I would detail all the activities for the week.

Each Sunday, I would erase the previous week's events and write down day by day what was happening for the week to come. Under each day, I'd write the main points in one color, then I would underline and mark the time in another color. This became the routine, week after week. Almost immediately I found that I no longer got questions about what was happening when. And if I did, I would often just point to the whiteboard instead of telling them.

In the beginning, there were a few Sundays when I didn't get to updating the week's calendar on the whiteboard, and the kids noticed. They had come to count on a visual calendar located in a place where they walked by all the time or would see it while they were eating. Sometimes, I layered in meal planning, too, but meal planning has never been my strong suit, so that seemed to be a harder one to keep track of. I would periodically put motivational quotes or ask questions for everyone to ponder. Often, in one corner, I would scribble a random list of grocery items that needed to be picked up.

Here's why the whiteboard with the weekly family schedule worked so well for us:

It was located in a place where it was seen regularly by everyone.

I was no longer the gatekeeper of the family calendar. The kids had accountability for knowing what was happening and when themselves.

There was less yelling because I didn't get frustrated with all their questions.

It kept us on track and on time.

The act of writing out the weekly schedule allowed me to see if there were any conflicts or things that needed to be figured out such as arranging rides to an activity or addressing any missing equipment that might be needed for something.

The kids had ownership for their weekly schedule. They knew they had to read what was going on and be ready for the day's agenda.

Did I mention less yelling?

Writing out the plan for the week is a practice that I have done in my personal notebook for years. It has helped me get clear on what is going on. Applying this method to our family schedule and putting the calendar in an easy-to-see place has been a key communication tool to keep us all on track. The biggest win has been a more harmonious house.

footprints.

➔ *How do you communicate in your house?*
➔ *Is it working for you?*
➔ *Is there something that you could implement to take the pressure off of you in your home?*

TRACKING YOUR PROGRESS

You need to track your progress so you can look back at where you've been and see where you are going. Intuitively, I knew this. I knew that if I kept track of how many words I wrote, I would be able to better track my progress along the way. But I continued to be inconsistent in writing. One week, I would blast through my word count goals, and another week barely touch fingers to keyboard. I was frustrated with myself.

When I committed to publishing my book and had a date on the calendar to hand in my first draft (ahh!), I knew that I needed to get serious about logging the words on the page. I set a goal to write 250 words per day. I knew that this was something that was achievable and could be done within the typical forty-five-minute writing session I would do each morning. I also knew that I would probably blow past that number, but the most challenging part for me would be to be focused enough as I sat down to write each day. Distraction is my nemesis, and with head-spinning speed, I can quickly get off track and that would be it for that particular writing session.

Just start. Have a rough idea of the topic you are writing on each day. Hide the phone. Put the music on and go. A new year provided a fresh start and new perspective to my writing quest. I set my word count goal per day, had put together a high-level outline and chapter summary for the book, and armed with this structured approach, I was never at a loss for a topic to write about each morning.

As with any new habit or routine, the first week I was full on. I wrote with fervor each morning. The words were pouring out of me. The energy continued into the second week. The third week the same. By week four, I was a writing machine. Writing in the morning had become for me what coffee in the morning was to others. I couldn't start my day without it.

I wouldn't say that I was addicted to seeing words on the page. That wasn't my motivation. Rather, it was the exercise of keeping track of how many words I would log each day. I had long kept an agenda where I planned my week. Now, each day, after I had completed my morning writing session, I would note how many words I had written: 562 on Monday, 841 on Tuesday, 778 on Wednesday, etc. At the end of the week, I would add up my word count and mark the total with a big bold circle on the page. I felt a sense of pride at how much I had written. So often I had set out to achieve something, but after a week or two found excuses why it wasn't working and just bailed.

This time was different. At first, I had become obsessed. But then I kept going, and it became just something I did. My motivation had originally been driven by not wanting to fail again and a determination to make it all work. This helped with my obsessive consistency the first few weeks. Writing down my word count each day and tallying it at the end of the week is what kept me going after the initial energy faded. I didn't want to miss a day. I was motivated to see that number at the end of the week. I loved looking back through my notebooks to see the numbers each week. I felt a sense of pride at my achievement.

Why was this time different?

For one, I had a deadline. I had a specific goal to work toward: my manuscript submission date. It was like I was training for a race on a certain date, and the work needed to be done ahead of time or I wouldn't be able to get through it.

Tracking my progress fueled my fire. It is what kept me going. On days when I didn't write as much as I had hoped, I promised myself that I would only have one day like that; then I would be back on track the next day. I allowed myself the grace to know that not every day was going to be a winner but also the structure to know that if I missed one day, I wouldn't miss the next. I got back on track, back to counting.

As I flip back through the pages of my notebook, I am proud of the progress I have made. I am determined to keep going. Determined to keep logging the words each morning. Step by step, my journey to becoming a writer was happening. Brick by brick. The book is being built.

footprints.

→ *What are things in your life you could track (and write down!) as a way to hold yourself accountable?*
→ *Consider regularly reviewing your progress.*
→ *Celebrate! Movement forward is a big deal!*

FINDING MY BOOKS—LITERALLY

He was awfully cute and pretty serious about school. In fact, the night I confessed to his roommate that I had a crush on Brad, I had barged into their house after a night at the bar and he was up late studying for a midterm exam. The next day I was a little embarrassed at my behavior and pretty sure he wouldn't call. But I was also impressed at his focus. Here it was a Saturday night and he had said no to going out with his friends. I am not sure I could have resisted the temptation.

Academic success had eluded me my first couple years in university. When I tried to study or write papers at home, I often wandered around and chatted with whoever was watching TV. When I went to the library to do research, I invariably found myself talking to someone I knew or getting distracted reading something that had nothing to do with why I was there.

It was moving into the final exam period for the year. I only had two exams and was up to my eyeballs in term papers. The expectations in university had kicked my butt so far, and I knew I couldn't just float through and do well. I needed to study. I needed to do the work. My boyfriend (yes, that cute studious one) and a couple of his roommates would often study at the engineering library where it was dead quiet. No one talked! You could hear a pin drop. At times, I wondered if anyone was alive there. One night, I decided to join them to see if I could concentrate better in a less distracting environment.

Lo and behold it worked. That first night at the engineering library I got more done than I had in three previous study sessions on my own.

I kept going back. Again and again. It was a bonus I got to see Brad, too!

I often had a short nap before I started studying. I would put my head down on the table for around fifteen minutes, shut my eyes, and power down my brain. When I woke, I would feel refreshed and ready to go. Brad and his friends thought this habit was hilarious. Who was this napping girl at the library?

One time, I woke from my power nap to find my books missing. They were gone. They couldn't have gone far, I thought. It is not like a bunch of engineers would want to read about Canadian judicial law procedures. The boys were starting to smile and chuckle. Ha, I realized. Those jerks had done something with my books. With a giggle I started to look around me.

"Warmer, warmer," one of them said.

Ah, we were playing a game of hot and cold with my books. I walked down one aisle and found one of the books.

"Colder, colder," the voice said again.

Eventually, I found all my books and got down to work.

This pattern happened again and again. Nap. Missing books. Giggles. They'd hide my books and I'd seek them. It was a thing. What had also become a thing was that I was actually getting work done. No wandering. No chatting. No getting up constantly for snacks. Pen to paper (this was pre-laptops!) and go. It turns out that one of the biggest things I had been missing was being surrounded by people who were motivated and focused on their work. They pulled me along by example.

I came to understand the power of being around other people who are similarly motivated. If I had been chatty and distracted, they would have told me to get lost. But because they got down to work, I had no choice but to do the same. I just had to find my books first.

footprints.

→ *Think back to times when the urge to quit was strong, but the people around you kept you going.*
→ *What helped then?*
→ *How can you recreate that support in other ways?*

POSITIVE ENERGY

Why is it so hard just to be genuinely happy for someone? It's a question I've asked myself when I feel hurt that someone I'm close to isn't as excited as I am. Or when I'm made to feel bad because I'm doing something that I am genuinely happy about. My initial reaction was to downplay my excitement to make them feel better. It took a long time for me to understand that their reaction wasn't about me; it was about them. How they were feeling. What was important to them.

To be clear, I am not talking about kicking someone while they are down and rubbing my own enthusiasm in their face. But even when you are feeling low or not so good about yourself, there is always an opportunity to react to someone's good news without making it about yourself.

Positive energy can be contagious if—and this is a big if—someone is open to reframing how they receive news in such a way that they encourage the other person and give them confidence. Seth Godin refers to this as "cooperative enthusiasm." He suggests that in the moment of receiving news about something, regardless of how you are feeling, your job could be to enthusiastically help bring out the very best version of the idea. Encourage the other person forward. "Perhaps positive thinking is contagious," he says. I couldn't agree more.

With that in mind, let's reframe some negative reactions that some people make when they hear someone else's happy news.

Me: I am so excited for the hiking trip Brad and I just booked. We leave in two weeks!

Them: Must be nice. I wish my husband and I would go away somewhere just the two of us. I'm so jealous.

Alternate conversation:

Me: I am so excited for the hiking trip Brad and I just booked. We leave in two weeks!

Them: That's great news. I hope you both have a wonderful time away together.

You can still be envious that your friend is going away and you aren't, but rather than squash their excitement, you can acknowledge how they are feeling without making it about you. When you tell someone you are jealous, the conversation comes to a screeching halt. Or at least it does with me. I never know how to respond.

Let's explore another example.

Me: When I see you on the weekend, I can hardly wait to show you the tattoo I just got!

Them: What? You got a tattoo? I didn't think you were into tattoos at all.

Alternate conversation:

Me: When I see you on the weekend, I can hardly wait to show you the tattoo I just got!

Them: You sound really excited. You'll have to tell me more about the design you decided on when we see each other.

Your friend might be thinking about the times you have ranted about tattoos and is assuming you are having some kind of midlife crisis. Or maybe they can't stand tattoos because their ex-boyfriend was covered in them. But instead of questioning your decision, they simply acknowledge that you seem excited and that they want to know more.

You don't have to agree with your friend, but you don't need to make it about how you are feeling or what is on your mind at that moment either. Sometimes saying less is the most meaningful thing you can do. It takes some practice to reframe your reaction, but trust me, it is worth it.

Enthusiasm and positive thinking can be contagious. The people you surround yourself with matter. "Cooperative enthusiasm" makes a difference. When I think about who I want to be around as I work toward something exciting in my own life, I will choose people who lift me up every time.

footprints.

→ *Who in your life supports your ideas and your successes?*

→ *Who is happy for you when you have news to share?*

→ *How do you react when others share their happy news with you?*

FINDING YOUR SUPPORT

Pandemic-land created this world where for what felt like forever, we could only connect with people online. Community and connection were suddenly limited to tiny boxes on our computer screens. At the start of the pandemic during the phase that we thought would only be two or three weeks to "flatten the curve" (ha!), there were virtual calls to connect with colleagues, family, friends, and for school. My book club got together on Zoom, and I even hosted a baby shower over Zoom when the family couldn't get together to celebrate.

After a few months of the frenzied Zoom world, we started to tire of only being able to meet with people via the little screen boxes. Socializing on Zoom sucked. The same voices would dominate the conversation, and the constant screens made me feel tired and even more disconnected from everyone. I had Zoom fatigue.

It was during this time that I focused more seriously on writing. In the darkness of the early morning, the words would flow out of me. Seeing my ideas and musings on the page and keeping track of my burgeoning word count motivated me to keep going. However, as I moved further along in my writing journey, I discovered that writing could be lonely. Just me, my ramblings, and my computer. Blink, blink, blink went the cursor. The white screen of the page just sat there waiting for me to fill it with my words and ideas. In my everyday life, I wasn't surrounded by other writers. I had no one else to connect with and share ideas. No one who understood the rush of being on a roll with your words. No one who could appreciate just how hard writing could be.

I had reached the point where I craved a supportive community to be around, and since the Universe seems to know just what we need when we need it, I was fortunate to be connected with a guided author program. Instinctively, I knew I needed to join this group. Even though the people in the group were scattered across North America, it was a collection of writers who met every week on Zoom for a writing and accountability call. Pretty quickly these Thursday calls became the best part of my week. We would each do a quick update at the start of the call, then mute our microphones, darken our screens, and write. At the end, we would all check in to see how the session went.

Even though I wasn't sitting in the same room as the other writers, just knowing that we were all writing at the same time made me feel connected and less alone. Sometimes, I would even look briefly at the Zoom screen while I was writing to see the others who were there and then go back to my writing knowing I had a supportive community around me. I was able to share with the group what I was excited about and ask for help or advice when I needed it. Collectively, we celebrated one another's wins, and I felt the power of the group every week.

I learned that when there is purpose in meeting online, in this case a writing group, the Zoom format worked. My first choice is always to meet with someone in person, but when you cannot find a like-minded community in your immediate surroundings, you can still find people who are working toward similar goals in a virtual world. We had a clear objective: connect and write.

It was through this supportive community that I was able to propel my writing forward and a big reason why you are reading this book today. It can take time, but once you find your people, the ones who cheer you on, the ones who hold space for you, and the ones who celebrate your wins, hang on tight. Who you surround yourself with matters.

footprints.

- ➤ *Think of times when you have been working on your own.*
- ➤ *How did it feel? Did you like it?*
- ➤ *Even when it seems like there is no one nearby, who could you find accountability with online?*

life happens

> "The work you put in to develop your habits provides the stability you need when things get tough."
>
> –Sarah Hepburn

Someone asked me the other day when I had been the most surprised in my life. The day I found out I was pregnant with twins was top of mind. I remember it like it was yesterday.

I had gone for a routine ultrasound when I was about thirteen weeks pregnant. As I lay there in the dimly lit room on the exam table waiting for the examination to start, I had been thinking about the upcoming baby's arrival and what it would mean for our life. I was thinking about work and how it would change my career. I was thinking about our house and wondering if it was big enough to bring a baby home. And I was thinking about how totally not ready I was for any of it.

I was relieved that I had nine months to get used to the idea of starting a family, but I was also very aware that my body already felt so different from before. I was exhausted, I could barely eat, and my middle was thick and had lost all shape.

The tech entered the room and said, "Let's get things started." As she began, she murmured, "Hmm . . ." followed by "Ahh . . ."

I turned my head to try to see the baby on the screen, but she had it turned away so I couldn't catch a peek.

Then she said the words that I never expected to hear: "Oh, you're having twins!"

"What?!" I said as I immediately sat up on the exam table.

"You're having twins." She calmly repeated what she had already said and gently pushed my shoulder so I would lie back down on the exam table.

As she started again with the ultrasound, I sat back up again, this time swatting the ultrasound wand out of her hand as I yell-sobbed (is that a thing?), "I didn't know I was having twins!"

"Oh!" She looked at me with wide eyes. "I just presumed you knew," she said with (maybe?) a hint of apology in her voice.

"Well. Clearly not," I stammered. At this point I was in shock. *Two babies? What was I supposed to do with two babies?*

I collected myself enough so she could continue the ultrasound. As I lay there, my mind was racing. I hadn't been ready to start a family with one baby—two babies wasn't even something I could fathom.

As I stumbled out of the ultrasound clinic into the bright July sunshine, I felt blinded. All the things I knew to be true about life had just changed. Not only was I about to become a mother, but I was to be a mother to two babies. At the same time. Bam, instant family.

In that moment, I knew I should call my husband and tell him the news. But I didn't want to. Even though I stood there holding an ultrasound picture that clearly showed two babies in my belly, I didn't want to make it real. In my shocked mind the ultrasound picture was of someone else's babies. If I called him and said the words out loud, it would be real. Right now it was all just an abstract moment in time.

I walked toward my car, overwhelmed by the news and what was to come. And scared of all the unknowns.

I pulled out my cell phone and dialed his number. "What's the craziest news I could tell you right now?"

"Ha ha. What? That we're having twins?" he joked at the other end of the line.

I stood there in the parking lot saying nothing. I stared at the nearby highway. The July sun felt relentless, and I could feel a trickle of sweat roll down the back of my neck. Tears poured down my face as I tried to find the words.

"Sarah? Sarah? Are you still there? Is everything okay?"

"I'm here," I finally said. "You guessed right. We are having twins. We are having two babies."

There was a pause on the other end of the phone. "Babe, we will figure this out. We have time to figure this out before the babies come. It will be okay."

I didn't know how to respond, so I just agreed with him. But in my heart, I knew everything was forever changed. I knew that I would have to learn to adapt to life's surprises in ways I never had before.

Two babies. Twins. As shocked as I was, I knew I would figure it all out. And I did.

footprints.

→ *When have you been the most surprised in your life?*
→ *How did you react?*
→ *How did it change you?*

FINDING KINDNESS FOR YOURSELF

In my teenage years, when I was training as an elite athlete, I knew how to listen to and understand my body. I would notice even the slightest of tweaks. This helped for training and managing injuries. Long after I retired from swimming, my heightened level of body intuition and awareness never left me.

I am hyper aware of every ache, pain, wheeze, twitch, and tremor. As I have gotten older, sometimes this has led to anxiety about my health. There's a pain in my side. Hmm . . . maybe there is a problem with my colon. I'm winded and having chest pains. Hmm . . . maybe I have an issue with my heart. There's a weird bump on my knee or a weird rash on my torso. Whatever could that be? At times, this awareness has indeed turned into something more with a recurrence of cellulitis infections over several years on my face and knee. But the pain in my side? Who knows. It settled down after a while. The chest pains? Got my heart checked out and all is good, strong, in fact. As are my lungs. I had those checked out at the same time as my heart, just to be sure.

I realize this sounds paranoid and tending toward hypochondria, but it isn't without history.

You see, all my life, I've been allergic to nuts. Allergic to a lot of things, actually, but the nut allergy has caused the most chaos. Growing up in the '70s and '80s, there wasn't a ton of nut awareness. In fact, there wasn't much awareness of any kind of allergies. I can remember eating a piece of Christmas cake when I was in grade two and instantly feeling sick from the walnuts in it. The cake looked good, and it didn't even occur to me that there were nuts in it. I didn't tell anyone, not even a teacher. Instead, I just stuck my fingers down my throat and puked in the classroom water fountain. Classy, right?! Also, gross. Then I went outside for recess as if nothing had happened.

For the longest time in my twenties and thirties, I would hear my body telling me something was going on. Sinus pain, debilitating exhaustion, or a weird rash. There were always whispers. Until my body got tired of whispering and something would explode. A massive sinus infection leading to bronchitis. The weird rash would turn out to be a skin cell infection that would require IV antibiotics.

Why did I ignore the subtle whispers? Why, when I was so prone to knowing and understanding the chatter of my body, would I hear it telling me that something was off and that I needed to rest or regroup, but I would just keep going? In hindsight, I think part of me didn't want to admit something was wrong. I didn't want to admit that perhaps my body wasn't working as well as I wanted it to. I didn't want to step off the hamster wheel and give my body what it needed to keep me going. I basically needed to be hit over the head with a mallet to actually stop.

With each infection, I would slip into a dark mood. They all seemed so random. I felt defective. There were all sorts of things I wanted to do, but my body was telling me no. At the time, I interpreted the signals to be that I wasn't strong enough, and I could never do the things I wanted. I started to jump at the slightest ache. I was paranoid about booking a trip, worried that it would be delayed or couldn't happen. I had to delay a trip to Arizona because I had swallowed a turkey bone that was in soup and had to have surgery to remove it. Really? I was eating soup! I was also wolfing it down as I raced around trying to get ready to leave the next morning. I wasn't paying attention as I ate. I was talking and moving around while gathering things I needed to go away. Always needing to be doing many things at the same time.

Working with a naturopath helped. She has been able to look beyond the surface symptoms and start to address some of the root causes such as low vitamin D and iron levels. It has been a collaborative relationship where I feel heard and we can talk through things together. I didn't have this type of relationship with my family doctor or the traditional medical community as my symptoms often weren't "bad enough." They would dismiss things as just something I would have to deal with.

At the core of it all, my body was telling me I needed to look after some other issues first before I could push it. I needed to slow down and listen to what it was saying. I needed to stop racing in life. I needed to be patient and kind to myself. Loving myself and loving my body for what it was is something I had struggled with all my life. When I started to slow down, I began to understand that the nicer I was to myself, the further I could go.

In slowing down and not trying to do a million things at one time, I am better about managing health issues before they get bad. I have been able to do more, once I peeled back the layers and got to the root cause of things.

It is not to say that I am still not prone to random infections, because those do pop up. A few years ago when I would get a bad sinus infection, I would slip into a dark depression for days, but now I know I need to be kind to my body and mind. I need rest (but not stay-in-bed-all-day-depressed rest). I need liquids and nourishing foods. Mindset is everything, and in knowing that I can love my body for all the amazing gifts it gives me is healing in and of itself.

footprints.

- When have there been times when you have been hard on yourself?
- How could you shift your thinking to find kindness for yourself?
- Do you listen to your inner voice with compassion?

YOUR INNER VOICE

It has taken a long time for me to understand that transformation starts with how you talk to yourself. Anything that is going to last starts with seeing what is good about your mind and body, and in finding gratitude for the gifts it gives you.

My health over the years has been a story of falling down and getting back up. I was living in a state of perpetual paranoia that something was going to happen, followed by waves of failure and disappointment when things didn't go according to plan because my mind was distracted or my body broke down.

Over the years, this frequent pattern of health flare-ups, treating the symptoms, never fully understanding the root cause, and being told that there was nothing of significance wrong with my body shattered my confidence. Because I have a high level of awareness of what is going on with my body, I always knew when something wasn't right. And yet it was never "bad" enough for doctors to look any further. The message I would hear is: You don't warrant help. Figure it out on your own. You are not "bad" enough for us to test any further.

I knew that things could be so much better. Regularly peeling skin and frequent joint aches shouldn't be something that I just needed to accept. Yet the message I received over and over was basically to deal with it.

When I asked for help it felt like it never came, so I would push and try to figure it all out on my own. I didn't feel like I could count on anyone but myself.

This cycle has been a theme throughout my life. I never knew when the next thing was going to happen, when the next flare was going to occur. It seemed like either my mind or my body was letting me down. I'd commit to doing something, only to have to renegotiate the deadline again because I was so distracted I never did the work. I'd make plans, but then I'd get sidelined again, this time because my body was telling me to fuck off.

It took me a while to listen to my inner voice, to the whispers that couldn't be ignored. For a long time, I didn't understand the connection between the body and the mind. I didn't understand that how I thought about my body would affect my ability to heal. I didn't listen or pay attention to the warning signs. Then bam, something would happen. Any time a rash or random infection would flare, I would spiral to a really dark place. It would be weeks before I felt healed again. My body was screaming at me to make a change.

I would love to write that I am a well-oiled machine in the prime of health and crushing big physical challenges, but that would be a lie. The random occurrences still happen. I am still figuring things out. I know there are still options I haven't explored. But what has changed is that I have found gratitude for my body and what it does for me.

Starting from a place of gratitude has shifted my perspective. No longer do I get down for days when something happens. No longer do I try to "push through it" like nothing is happening. I listen. I am patient. I've slowed down. I know that with a calm, loving, rested approach, it will all pass. I will continue to try to solve the puzzle, but in the meantime, I feel an immense sense of gratitude for where I am at.

I often say this to myself:

Thank you, body. Thank you for your love. For your gifts. Thank you for all you do for me. I promise to do
everything I can to nurture and heal you. I promise to listen to your signs. I love you. Thank you for
everything you have enabled me to do.
My body. My heart. My soul.
Breathe in. Breathe out.

footprints.

→ When have you been kind to yourself?

→ When have you been overly harsh?

→ How could you shift the conversation you have internally with yourself to be kind and gentle?

A LOVE LETTER

Have you ever written a love letter to yourself? Have you ever listed all the things you love about yourself? Have you ever told your future self what you want to know? A few years ago, I wrote a love letter to myself. I smile as I read it now and want to share it with you.

> *Dear future Sarah,*
>
> On the occasion of your birthday this weekend, I made you a list of things that you have learned in recent times, things that have kept you grounded, and things that spark joy. When your memory starts to go in your old age, just take a peek back and see what worked for you in your midforties. We all could use a little cheat sheet, after all.
>
> So, in no particular order, here are some things to keep in mind as you move forward in life:

- Objects in motion stay in motion. Keep moving. Keep putting one foot in front of the other, even when you don't want to. You can never get stuck as long as you are in motion.
- Swearing is perfectly acceptable. Always. Don't let anyone tell you otherwise.
- Move your body for at least thirty minutes a day. Get the workout in. Get out for a hike. As the old Nike slogan says: "Just Do It." You, Sarah, are a nicer person to everyone around you when you have gotten your sweat on each day.
- Zits happen in your midforties. Get over it. (But seriously, what the actual F*%&?!)
- Hug often. Hug always. I'm talking the hold tight and breathe together squeezey-type of hug. The energy shared is magic.
- Teenagers are the best. They aren't always easy, but they are awesome. Laugh at dinner. Dance wildly together in the car. Fart with confidence (they are stinky boys after all). Hang out. You are building the foundation for your relationship with your boys in the years to come.
- Ask for what you want in life. Always. As Wayne Gretzky said: "You miss 100 percent of the shots you don't take." Take the damn shot. Just ask.
- This too shall pass. Always. Nothing is permanent.
- Wearing hiking boots and leopard print flats in the same day is totally a thing. You can be covered in mud one minute and classy the next.

* *Be nice to your body. It has carried you through a lot. Feed it well. Fill it with water. Avoid the things you know will make it grumpy. The occasional indulgence is encouraged, but make it a treat, a whoopsie you might say, and get back on track the next day.*
* *Put the reps in. You aren't going to get what you want by sitting on your butt, Sarah. All it takes is one rep. Then another. Then another. Keep going.*
* *Sleep is your superpower. You know how to sleep soundly and anywhere. If the day has been crap, go to bed. Things are always better in the morning.*
* *When you are stressed, ask yourself what is the worst thing that could happen. It is never as bad as it seems, and there is always a way forward.*
* *Let loose once in a while and dance your ass off. Bonus points if you find a stage or table to dance on.*
* *If something is bothering you or has made you mad, wait twenty-four hours before reacting. Gather your thoughts. Think about what you really want to say. When you speak in anger, the message is lost.*
* *You thrive when you consistently rock your morning routine. Get up early. Meditate. Stretch. Journal. Watch the sunrise.*
* *Keep doing things that scare you. Growth doesn't happen when you are comfortable.*
* *Be silly. Be playful. Laugh until you cry and pee your pants. Let that big smile loose.*
* *The word "should" is a swear word. Never use it in a sentence from this moment forward.*

* At the end of the day, the only thing you can control in life is how you act and how you react. Control what you can. Life will unfold as it may.
* Love hard. Be kind. Be curious. Be unapologetically you.

> Love,
> Sarah of the here and now

footprints.

→ What do you want your future self to know?
→ When have you needed reminders of what makes you awesome?
→ Write a love letter to yourself.

WORDS MATTER

As I've said, I have written in a journal since I was young. Sometimes, it is a running dialogue of what I did the day before. Other times, it has been a rant of what is bothering me and what I am upset about. My journal is a safe place for me to say all the things I might never say out loud.

I have tinkered with different formats over the years. I write about my dreams. I tuck away notes and ideas that I want to explore another time. I have poured my feelings onto the pages in an unedited essay of emotion. I always feel better after writing.

When I'm experiencing a difficult time, I turn to my journal and begin madly writing to express how I am feeling. It helps. Usually after a deep journal session, I would feel sorted again. But the darkness was never far from the surface. When I would look back at what I had written during the darker times, things I had poured onto the pages were thoughts and feelings I would never say out loud.

My journal has always been my sacred space to vent. In recent years I started to consider that maybe the manner in which I was venting was actually perpetuating the negative feelings. Maybe by giving those feelings space and oxygen I was enabling them to stay alive and grow. I am not sure why it took so long for me to realize this. After all, when I am talking to others it drives me bonkers when the tone of the conversation is regularly negative. I think, geez, they really are just happy to sit in their own shit sandwich, aren't they? If I am so annoyed when I hear others speaking negatively, why was I so ready to speak to myself that way?

I read some of the passages that I had written over the past few years in my journal. I noticed a pattern. Massive gratitude followed by "down in the dumps, the world is ending" feelings. Extreme highs and super lows. What if I could somehow smooth out that curve a little, I thought. I still needed the space to feel my feelings, but did I need to go to the dark lengths I was going to express myself? Probably not.

I consciously started to shift my tone.

I still used my journal as a place to vent and feel all the big feelings. But now I write from a place of kindness. Not gooey positivity but kindness. I still share my frustration. I still express how I am feeling. But I use words that are kinder to myself as I write. For example, at one point in the pandemic, I was feeling pretty down when I tested positive for Covid. All I could think of was that I had done all the things I was "supposed" to do. Truth be told, I did feel like shit with a super bad head cold, chills, and a wicked headache, so I might have been forgiven for tumbling down a hole of despair, but I knew that I didn't want to feel that way. So I wrote a love letter to myself. I acknowledged how I was feeling. I acknowledged the frustration and the anger and the isolation and the "why me" feelings. Then I wrote to myself how grateful I was that my body was strong and could weather storms. I wrote about how grateful I was for sleep and warm mugs of lemon water and working out. I wrote about how I was grateful that I had been putting in the work to build my physical strength with a new weight training program. I acknowledged the shitty feelings, but then I reminded myself of all the good that surrounded me.

It worked. I needed that release in the love letter to myself. I needed to write down how I was feeling and get through it all.

It has taken time to evolve the conversation with myself. My journal continues to be my sacred space to explore my ideas and my feelings, but I am mindful of the words I am using and how I speak to myself.

footprints.

→ *What do you write in your journal?*
→ *Do you feel better or worse after your journal session?*
→ *Read through journal entries from the past months. What patterns do you notice? Do you write to yourself with love?*

WHEN MY BODY SAYS ENOUGH

I used to wonder at what point I would finally remember what happens when I indulge too often. When would I remember that if I had the bread and the greasy food and the cookies, something would inevitably happen with my skin, my joints, my mind, and my body.

My face was pretty bad. Not the worst it had been but definitely in the top five occurrences of "random shit that explodes on Sarah's face." When I traced back over the preceding weeks I knew I hadn't been kind in how I fueled myself. I had forgotten that a little bit here and a little bit there adds up to a lot of what my body doesn't like. My glasses were dirty with flakes of skin, I could feel the itch and burn on the left side of my face, and my neck felt like sandpaper. Gross, I know. I gag reading those words! I would love to say this was new but nope. I've just learned to roll with it.

Now, when random infections appear, I'm offering myself a deeper level of kindness and understanding. I no longer feel as defeated and disappointed in my body as I did in the past. I don't feel like a failure that I can't eat whatever everyone else does. I'm not beating myself up for occasionally falling prey to old habits that no longer serve me. I'm trying not to eat my frustrations and ignore the repercussions that come from bingeing.

As I applied the cream and gently wiped my peeling face with a washcloth, I found myself offering my raw skin words of encouragement: *This too shall pass and it will all be okay.*

While I still fall prey to temptation of habits from years past, it happens less frequently, and I am accepting things for what they are when they do happen. For me, this is a giant step forward. There is a lesson to be learned even when things are really hard. My burning, flaky skin is reminding me that there is work still to be done. Even when it is raw and sore, I am grateful to my skin for the chaotic lessons it continues to offer.

footprints.

→ *What have you been tempted by?*

→ *How does your body react?*

→ *How do you talk to yourself when your body doesn't work as well as you hope?*

habits provide calm in chaos

> "Tough times never last, but tough people do."
> –Robert H. Schuller

One thing I've learned is that strong habits are built when things are good and are tested during hard times. **The work you put in to develop your habits provides the stability you need when things get tough.** This was something I came to understand one March after a winter of deep hibernation.

The winter had been quiet. Borderline boring, in fact. Not many plans in the evenings. Our social life was slow. I focused on my sleep and woke at the same time each day. I meditated, wrote in my journal, met my daily writing word count goals, and worked out—all before the rest of the house got going each day.

The quiet of the winter had afforded me the opportunity to really get clear on what worked and repeat it. Day after day. It sounds monotonous, but it wasn't. In the dark of the winter, I found comfort in what I did each morning to start my day. I started to notice that I was focusing better throughout the day. I wasn't craving crappy food like I had before. At times, I almost felt like I was buzzing with energy. On the rare days that I didn't run my full morning routine, I just didn't have the same pep. Truthfully, I didn't expect the shift to be so dramatic.

I kept doing what I had been doing. On repeat. Day in, day out. All of January. All of February. Getting ample sleep at night and running through my morning routine with my headphones on to block out any distractions were sacred to me. It might have seemed borderline obsessive, but I was feeling so good throughout the rest of the day I kept going.

Then the March break came, and we went away on a ski holiday. I continued to focus on my morning routine. I rose before everyone else and meditated, stretched, wrote in my journal, and worked toward my daily writing goals. I felt really good that I was able to still make it all happen, even on holiday. It was just what I did at that point. All the daily habits that I had been focusing so hard on during those dark winter months were just what I did in the morning now.

As with any habit, it will be tested, and often you don't know when that will be. The test of my morning routine came when one of my older sons had a bad ski accident and had to have emergency surgery. It was scary. There were so many unknowns. But as I found myself waiting in the hospital for him to be operated on or sitting by his bedside in recovery, I pulled out my headphones and did a short guided meditation. I had my journal with me and wrote a few lines of gratitude. I found ways to stretch and move my body in the hospital. It wasn't a full workout, but I got my blood flowing.

When life sent me sideways, I was able to find strength in the things that had kept me going all winter. I focused on gratitude through my meditation and journal passages. I moved my body. I ate food that would fuel me. It would have been so easy to let it all go and completely understandable given the circumstances, but I didn't. I knew that to be the best support for my son, I needed to be my best. And the way I knew how to be my best was to keep doing the things that gave me energy.

As the days went on, my habits were the one thing that was consistent and predictable. This grounding helped to support both of us during a really scary time.

It was the first true test of my daily habits. And I knew that I was on to something. Writing notes of gratitude in my journal helped me drown out the worry, stress, and noise from people around me and the messages that were pinging away on my phone. I was able to stay in a positive, forward-looking headspace and not slip into a negative place. I was able to remind myself that eating a bag of chips for dinner would not help me, and I chose foods that would nourish me in the days ahead. Small decisions added up.

It was a reminder to me that you don't just do something every day for the sake of doing it. You don't just go through the motions. A habit is something that you can use to drive yourself forward, to support yourself when you need it. A habit has purpose. Before my son's ski accident, I had already felt the energy and focus that was coming with my morning routine. When he was in hospital, I found strength and comfort in my daily habits. I was able to find stability in doing what I knew would give me energy and allow me to focus on what I needed to focus on that day.

For me, it was a powerful lesson in why habits matter. And that I have the power to shape my habits to drive myself forward.

footprints.

→ *When have your daily habits been tested?*
→ *Take a moment to reflect on how you handled things when life didn't go as you expected.*
→ *What did you learn from that experience?*

HABITS AND ROUTINES WILL EVOLVE

Habits do and should evolve. You are human, after all. Once you have established a habit, you can build on it. Runners don't start by running a marathon. They start by walking around the block. Then running for one minute and walking the next minute. The stretches of running get longer from there. Start simple and build on your foundation.

Recognize that life happens. There are going to be days when you stay up later than you'd like. There are going to be days when you miss your workout. And there are going to be days when you yell at your kids. If you miss a day or screw up, promise yourself that it is only one day. Start fresh again looking forward instead of beating yourself up for missing one day.

Just as certain parenting habits, like bedtime, had to evolve as my three boys grew up and transitioned from toddlers to kids to teens, I also had to change the way we communicated. Once I stopped pestering them to follow certain rules (like showering before bed because, hello, stinky boys!), a funny thing happened. They actually started showering on their own initiative. Was it because they were sitting in their own filth (again, teen boys!)? Or maybe because I wasn't nagging anymore? I had stopped trying to control the situation and the kids learned on their own that they actually do like being clean.

We talked. I shared what was bothering me at a time when tempers weren't flared. For us, this was during dinner when we were all together. I told the boys what was on my mind. I asked them to share how they were feeling. They told me they didn't like being nagged to do something. I told them that the clutter in the house and the constant arguing about showering and going to bed was exhausting me. It was a calm discussion. Everyone felt like their feelings had been heard. We agreed to make some changes.

The conversation was a turning point. No longer was I fully in charge or in control. Even though I was the grown up, and I suppose technically had the final word, the kids all felt like their opinions mattered simply because I asked. It was an example for us all to be collaborative, respectful, considerate, and kind.

Looking back, I am reminded that routines are not permanent. Routines need to adapt and shift as life does. Sometimes the transition period is messy, but a willingness to acknowledge that something isn't working is key to making change.

You don't always know when and how things are going to evolve. You just need to be open to it when it comes. For my family, we could have continued to drift through and yell and be frustrated with one another, but instead we chose to be deliberate about what changes needed to happen to work for everyone.

The most effective way to create change and respect was to start with a simple conversation. From there I was able to say, "Hey, remember what we talked about? Has something changed that we need to tweak?"

footprints.

- ➔ *When routine needed to change in your house, what did you do?*
- ➔ *Is there something you could have done differently?*
- ➔ *What did you learn moving forward?*

walking forward

> "I'll never know. And neither will you,
> of the life you don't choose."
>
> –Cheryl Strayed

Some of my favorite hiking I have ever done has been in beautiful British Columbia. There is something about the mountains that energize me. I am reminded of just how small we really are in the world and how rooted in the land our history is. Every step on the trail is different as it weaves through the towering trees past lakes, rivers, and sprays of cold glacial water. The mountains are both beautiful and harsh with constant reminders of how fragile life can be.

Several years ago, I was with a very good friend of mine for a girls' getaway weekend in the Rockies. It was mid-June and still early hiking season in the mountains. Some trails were still snow covered while others were closed because of bear activity. We consulted with the local Parks Canada office and the original hike we had planned was closed due to avalanche risk. Instead, they recommended a hike a little further south in Kootenay National Park. It promised to be a difficult six-hour loop with a 1,055 m elevation gain that would have us climb up to spectacular alpine vistas and back down beside the Sinclair Creek. This sounded perfect to us. Off we set to the trailhead.

We were a little later setting out than we would have liked, but with it being close to the summer solstice, we knew we would have light until 10 p.m. which would leave us plenty of time (in theory!). We were prepared with maps and trail guides, a GPS, lots of food and water, layers of clothing, and bear spray. This was going to be epic!

My friend was in much better shape than I was as she zipped up the trail while I huffed and puffed behind her. The trail started in the trees and wound its way up. And up. And up. And . . . up some more. I was having moments of wondering what the fuck had I gotten myself into, but I started to find my groove and was rewarded after about an hour and a half of hiking when the trail opened up to a wide-open view of the mountains. We continued our ascent climbing past the treeline where the trail opened into a spectacular alpine meadow. I felt like I was on top of the world. We navigated a narrow path along the side of the peak and had a moment at the top celebrating and taking pictures. The wind was blowing and it was near freezing at the top, but we made it!

As we paused at the summit, I was pretty tired but looked forward to pointing my legs downhill as my quads and calves were killing from the climb up. Our map directed us to follow the treeline for about fifteen minutes, at which point we would drop into the forest and the main trail would start again. Except we couldn't find the trail. There was no cairn or trail marker as we had expected. We had gone too far to retrace our steps, so we continued down the mountain knowing we needed to connect with Sinclair Creek to find the trail and lead us out to the road. By now we were pretty nervous. Not only were we lost, but there was a ton of bear scat, and we had seen three sets of fresh bear tracks. We were in grizzly country, and we felt like they were all around us.

Once we connected with the "creek" (more like a river in places), we followed it downstream hopping from side to side and bushwhacking our way through. There was no trail. We were going on instinct, using our compass and marking our GPS points to keep track. At one point, we came to a canyon where the rocks rose high above the edge of the creek. The only way around was to climb up and over navigating mossy rocks and unsure footing. I don't know what I would have done without my friend at this point. Getting to the other side of the canyon had left me feeling spent, but she told me to buck up and keep moving. It was now 8 p.m., and we were rapidly running out of daylight. It was a weird moment to realize that the only way off the trail was under our own power. No one was coming to rescue us. And it was getting dark. We had to push on and find the path again.

Push on we did. The bush whacking was intense, jumping over brush and breaking down paths as we went. I was soaked. My legs were cut and bruised. I was covered in mud, but amazingly my body found another gear. I found the energy to keep going. I could only think of moving forward. We came around a corner, and like a blinking beacon, the trail appeared. Screaming with joy, we quickly moved down the path while blowing our whistles, singing, and making lots of noise so we wouldn't surprise the grizzlies we knew were lurking close by in the woods. It was about 9:30 p.m. at this point, and in the trees, the light was dim. We finally made it back to the highway where we were able to hitchhike the remaining 1.5 km to our car.

We had done it! At times, we didn't think we would find our way, but we did. We had the mental fortitude to persist and found another gear physically to propel us forward.

People often ask me what I like about hiking, and while the story I just shared is perhaps a more extreme example, the lessons I have learned on the trail are similar regardless of where I am. Hiking is consistently putting one foot in front of the other. It is you—and only you—that can propel yourself forward. When you fall, you have no choice but to pick yourself up and keep moving.

Sometimes, you don't always know where the path is, but you trust your intuition knowing that as you continue forward, the path will reveal itself when it is meant to. **There is always a way forward—on the trail and in life.**

One of the cardinal rules of hiking is to never hike alone. Always find the people who challenge you, the people who cheer you on when you need it most, and the people who will help you propel yourself forward. I never could have gotten through that grueling hike without my friend that day. It was truly a team effort.

Hiking can be hard. Life can be hard. But you never give up. You take a deep breath, dig in, and find another gear. And best of all, is the feeling of exhilaration knowing that you just challenged yourself. You tested your limits and went further than you thought. You grew as a person.

footprints.

→ *Has there been a time when your limits have been tested?*
→ *What did you learn about yourself?*
→ *Were you alone or with other people? What worked?*

LESSONS LEARNED ON THE TRAIL

Do I have it all figured out? Hardly. I could report that I am the queen of habits and am rocking every aspect of my life, but that would be total bullshit. I am human, and being human means I fall down from time to time. Often this happens when I am tired or things are too busy. The difference from the past and now is that if I do get off track, I now have the knowledge and confidence to pause, assess what is going on, and get going again. In other words, the recovery time is shorter.

Take exercise for example. In the past, I started and stopped various workout programs. Now, exercise is such an entrenched part of my daily routine I barely know a day without moving my body. Usually, I exercise for about thirty to forty-five minutes each day. Sometimes longer, sometimes shorter. But I always move my body. I figured out that the start of the day is when consistent exercise happens and when I work out at home I rarely miss. I don't always want to, but I always feel better after working out. On the occasion that I miss a day for whatever reason, I never miss two in a row, as I have said. That is the promise I have made to myself—and I'm keeping it!

When I've been able to identify why I do something and who I want to be, I am much more likely to stick with something. In the exercise example, I see myself as a fit, active person. To be fit and active means to move my body with purpose every single day.

LOOKING FORWARD

The more I have come to understand myself, the more I now know why I have always relied on habits and routine in my daily life. To most people, I am organized and on top of things. Heck, I used to run a team of people who specialized in building processes so things would run better at a bank. But the reality is habits have kept me from spinning. **Habits have minimized the chaos in my mind and my body.**

When I started to pay attention to the whispers and paused long enough to understand why I did what I did, I started to get clear on who I was and what I really wanted. I realized that habits weren't just something to use as a coping mechanism, habits could be used strategically to propel me forward.

Peeling back the layers of Sarah and figuring out who was still there was what started the transformation. Over time, I had played the roles of daughter, wife, mother, sister, friend, and colleague; and I didn't really know who the "real" Sarah was. Was she still there, inside? Where did she go? I was always filled with thoughts of "I should act like this" or "I should do this." Rarely did I ask myself if it was what I wanted or what was best for me. The implications of trying to please and look after so many people in my life were showing up in my health, my parenting, my relationships, and my ability to manage stress.

At one time, my journal pages told a story of a woman full of regret for the life she was living, of a woman who was lonely. Of a woman full of dreams of the life she thought she would be living, not the very different one she actually was. She felt small in her life and paralyzed to make change and move forward. She seemed almost tortured. Tortured with resentment. Tortured with regret. Tortured with self-loathing that she could not find a way forward.

Those words are different now, thankfully. It took time, and it was scary. But now the journal pages tell a story of gratitude and of letting go, of love and of joy. There are still the occasional dark words but never the deep holes of despair from years past.

As I write these words, I pause and look at the photo of my ten-year-old self I keep in my journal. I see her deep brown eyes, dark hair, striped summer dress and how she is smiling directly at the camera. My ten-year-old self believed blindly in a bright future. She had big dreams and no limits on what she could imagine and do.

I turn my eyes to the other photo I keep in my journal. It is a photo of forty-six-year-old me. It was taken on a hiking trip in the mountains. I can remember being red-faced and sweaty as I paused to have the photo taken. I was panting. We had been on a particularly difficult section of switchbacks, and my friend took the photo to both capture the stunning view and (I'm pretty sure) take a break. My hands are on my hips. I have my trusty backpack with me and a massive smile on my face. I look content. My eyes are bright. I am in my element, as they say.

I place the two photos in front of me side by side. The faces are the same: smiling directly at the camera. Calm. Confident. Strong. I know I want to feel that way even when I am not hiking. I want to feel that way even on a day when it doesn't feel like I can move forward. It is a reminder to me that to do the things I want to do in life it all starts with belief in myself. How I see and believe in myself is the foundation for everything.

If you start with any of the lessons in this book, start with believing in yourself. Everything else will follow from there.

I now help other women use the power of habit as a tool to weather life's storms and get what they want out of their one precious life. I encourage them to peel back the layers. Be confident in the person who is hiding inside. Be kind. I remind my clients that life isn't linear, but they can choose every day to wake up and keep moving.

As I sign off, my wish is for you to walk forward to create a life you love. Leverage the power of habit to navigate the inevitable chaos of life . . . one step at a time.

with gratitude
(a.k.a. acknowledgments)

I always thought writers were solitary creatures. They were people who hid in remote cottages deep in the woods and went into town once a week for provisions. Writers would spend hours typing on their laptops whilst periodically gazing at the birds and deer outside their window. Writers were like Colin Firth's character in the movie *Love Actually* who, after heartbreak, locks himself away in a cottage in the South of France to write his next novel and (spoiler!) discovers love again in the process.

The real truth about writing a book is that it takes a village. I don't say that lightly. I had always thought of myself as a writer, but I didn't write for a long time. A few years ago I challenged myself to write five hundred words per day. This led to sharing stories on my personal blog. I called these Essays and Letters because it created a softer, deeper connection with people than a blog might.

Sharing my story with others helped me find my voice in a way like never before. Without everyone who read and cheered me on, you wouldn't be holding this book in your hands today.

Thank you to Sabrina Greer and the Author Generator program. The community of authors you fostered lifted each other up and kept me going even when I wasn't so sure what I was doing! To the rest of the team at YGT Media including Doris, Michelle, and Christine—thank you for everything you've done throughout this process. And to Kelly, my editor, your kindness, encouragement, and help in shaping this book was exactly what I needed.

Mom, you taught me what home means—literally and figuratively. You've been by my side at my darkest times and showed me that with a little grace, humor, and tenacity anything is possible. Your lunch bag notes got me started on my letter writing journey.

Dad, steady hand. Always. You showed me what determination and laser focus looks like. I love that I can always find a book you'll enjoy and that I will steal it after you are done. I'm grateful we had all those car rides home from the pool but am still disappointed Mom found out how we'd been walking the dog each night.

My sisters, Katie and Lindsey, for always loving me for exactly who I am.

To Jean and George and Amy, you have always supported me and cheered me on unconditionally.

Lindsey Walker and Christina Crowe, you came into my life when I doubted the ability of my body and mind to heal. Both of you, in your own way, changed that and I am forever grateful.

My Irish Sisters, thank you for planting the seeds so many years ago in our tiny cottage in Ballyvaughan, and to Erik for sharing your wisdom and teaching me how to convert miles to kilometers on our hikes.

Philip McKernan, you pushed me in ways I never thought possible. Thank you for helping me remember just who Sarah is and pointing out that the prison cell door is open—I just have to walk through it. Working with you changed my life.

Jenn Walker, you were the most unexpected and powerful human to walk into my world. Your Jedi mind tricks launched me into another galaxy.

Mrs. Watson, my high school English teacher whose class I never skipped even after she busted me reading a Danielle Steele novel under my desk. Her energy, love of language, and sarcastic humor inspired my love of reading and writing all those years ago.

To my dear AF who I could always count on to comment on every essay I ever published—your wisdom and unabashed cheerleading is so missed.

My boys, thank you for loving me unconditionally. You are my biggest why, and I will always and forever be in your corner.

Brad, it is hard to put into words my gratitude for you. You are my best friend, my rock, and my most trusted advisor. I can hardly wait to see where we go next. I love you.

And finally, to the books I have read all my life and the authors who penned them. You were my escape, my friends, my school, and my dreams. I will forever love disappearing into your pages.

Much love,

sarah.

resources and works cited

(in alphabetical order)

Brené Brown, *I Thought It Was Just Me (but it isn't): Making the Journey from "What Will People Think?" to "I Am Enough"* (Avery, 2007).

Cheryl Strayed, *Tiny Beautiful Things: Advice on Love and Life from Dear Sugar* (Vintage, 2012).

Helen Keller, 1980, *Helen and Teacher: The Story of Helen Keller and Anne Sullivan Macy* by Joseph P. Lash, Chapter: On the Vaudeville Circuit, Start Page 487, Quote Page 489, A Merloyd Lawrence Book: Delacorte Press/Seymour Lawrence, New York. (Verified on paper)

James Clear, *Atomic Habits: An Easy & Proven Way to Build Good Habits & Break Bad Ones* (Penguin, 2018).

Philip McKernan, https://philipmckernan.com/

Rich Roll, https://www.richroll.com/

Robert H. Schuller, *Tough Times Never Last, but Tough People Do!* (Bantam, 1984).

Sarah Hepburn, https://www.sarahhepburn.ca/

Seth Godin, https://seths.blog/

William A. Ward, 1963 May 17, *Oklahoma City Star*, Page Title: Pennsylvania Avenue Methodist Church, Post Script, Quote Page M-110, Column 1, Oklahoma City, Oklahoma. (Newspapers_com)

YGTMedia Co. is a blended boutique publishing house for mission-driven humans. We help seasoned and emerging authors "birth their brain babies" through a supportive and collaborative approach. Specializing in narrative nonfiction and adult and children's empowerment books, we believe that words can change the world, and we intend to do so one book at a time.

🌐 ygtmedia.co/publishing
📷 @ygtmedia.company
f @ygtmedia.co